The Observer's Pocket Series

AUTOMOBILES

About the Book

With this latest edition *The Observer's Book of Automobiles* celebrates its Silver Jubilee as the outstanding pocket-size reference book of the automotive scene, providing illustrations and data of the world's most significant production cars. In this the 25th edition maximum coverage has been devoted to those models which have either been presented for the first time or changed in specification for 1981-82.

The book has been compiled with both the enthusiast and the professional in mind and has been designed to meet the needs of anyone requiring a handy volume containing concise information and clear illustrations for quick identification and reference.

About the Author

John Blunsden is one of Britain's foremost motoring writers with a career as an author, journalist, broadcaster, editor and publisher spanning more than 25 years and embracing all aspects of the motoring scene. Currently Chairman—for the second time—of the Guild of Motoring Writers and a founder member of the International Racing Press Association, he now devotes much of his time to the world of motoring books as Managing Director of Motor Racing Publications Ltd (publishers) and Connoisseur Carbooks (specialist booksellers) and as a consultant to other publishing houses in the motoring book field.

The Observer's Book of

AUTOMOBILES

Compiled by
JOHN BLUNSDEN

Charlotte Wake

FREDERICK WARNE
LONDON

First Edition 1955
Twenty-fifth Edition 1982

NOTE

The specifications contained in this book were collated on the basis of material available to the compiler up to the beginning of October 1981. All information is subject to change and/or cancellation during the course of the model year. Although every effort has been made to ensure correctness in compiling this book responsibility for inaccuracies and omissions cannot be accepted by the compilers and publishers.

LIBRARY OF CONGRESS CATALOG
CARD NO. 62–9807

ISBN 0 7232 1627 4

Typeset by CCC, printed and bound in
Great Britain by William Clowes (Beccles) Limited,
Beccles and London

1656.1181

INTRODUCTION

Regular readers of *The Observer's Book of Automobiles* will be aware that the presentation of data in this latest edition follows the pattern established over the past two years, when certain changes were made in an effort to make this very popular reference book an even more interesting and useful guide to the cars on our roads.

Inevitably it is impossible to cover the entire spectrum of world production of cars within the compass of less than 200 pages, and it has been necessary to be selective in the choice of entries. In doing so, prime importance has been given to those cars which have been introduced during the past year or so, as well as those which have undergone significant changes in specification during that period. At the same time, those models which have continued virtually unchanged have not been overlooked where they represent an important segment of the total market.

In these days most manufacturers design and produce cars for export sales as much as for their home market, and often specifications have to be changed to meet local demands and regulations. As far as possible, where a car is available on the British market it is the UK specification which has been quoted, even though this may be at variance with the specification in the country of manufacture. Not all of the models described and illustrated, however, are available in the UK, but such cars as have been included despite this have earned an entry because of their significance to the world automotive scene as a whole.

The period between the 'signing off' of a new car for production and its appearance in the showrooms is considerably longer than that between the passing of a book for press and its appearance on the bookshelves. Consequently, a number of models which might otherwise have been featured in this edition have had to be omitted either because they have yet to be revealed to the public, or because the relevant data on them was not available at the time this book went to press. Similarly, other cars which ordinarily would have warranted an entry have been excluded because of a pending change of specification which would have made the entry obsolete.

As competition between rival manufacturers intensifies there is a growing trend towards the marketing of 'limited edition'

5

versions of their regular product lines, which often offer better value for money and a higher-than-usual specification. For the most part these variants have been ignored, unless there has been a strong chance of their conversion into a long-term selling line.

In preparing the data which is published on the following pages considerable help has been provided by the manufacturers and/or their importers or concessionaires concerned, for which the author and publishers are most grateful. It is only whilst researching data of this type, however, that one discovers the degree to which inconsistencies have crept into factual material which has been assembled over the years.

For example, not every manufacturer uses precisely the same method of horsepower calculation, and confusion is compounded in conversion from metric to imperial measures, or vice versa, in so far as there are subtle differences in the DIN and ISO 1585 International Standards used for these calculations and conversions. In all cases it will be found that the output and torque figures quoted (in both metric and imperial units) in this book are either those obtained from factory sources or calculations which approximate very closely indeed to them.

Another area of considerable discrepancy concerns overall dimensions and unladen weight, the former, perhaps, because small changes in things like bumpers and side rubbing strips are seemingly ignored in certain quarters, and the latter because once again there is an inconsistency in the method of measurement. The figures quoted have been taken as the most accurate available, and should be found to be within acceptable tolerances.

One final word of advice. The specification of seemingly unchanging cars is usually undergoing subtle improvement all the time, and manufacturers will never lose the opportunity to uprate their cars whenever they can afford to do so. Conversely, in an effort to contain prices in an inflationary economic climate, car producers will occasionally 'detune' the specification of certain of their models. It is advisable, therefore, when using this book as a guide to car purchase, as distinct from a means of expanding one's interest in cars generally, to augment it with the latest sales literature obtainable from the relevant dealer. Meanwhile, events in the car-manufacture world will be monitored very closely during the coming year, for even as this book comes off the printing presses some of the content of the next edition of *The Observer's Book of Automobiles* is already being assembled.

The year in retrospect

The recession which the world's motor industry found so damaging in 1980 continued to stagnate demand throughout much of 1981, yet not for the first time the industry was able to put on a brave face in a daunting economic climate. Indeed, so severe were the financial and economic problems throughout much of the Western world that there was a considerable feeling of relief that the car market remained tolerably buoyant and in some areas actually showed a modest improvement over 1980 levels. The depth of the recession, however, had confirmed the fears of the most pessimistic forecasters and by the end of the year there was widespread belief within the industry that full recovery would not be achieved before 1983 at the very earliest.

Meanwhile, the industry's ability to ride out the storm was highlighted at the biennial Frankfurt motor show, where not only was there a wide selection of new or nearly new products on display, seemingly ideally suited to today's energy-conscious needs, but some of the most influential manufacturers went to great efforts to reveal at least some of their forward thinking through a fascinating selection of project cars depicting the motoring scene through the closing years of the 20th century. By the year 2000, it is now becoming clear, the ratio of car performance to fuel consumption will have improved so dramatically as to delight the owner/driver and the environmentalist alike, and the first steps along this road have already been taken.

Perhaps inevitably in a 'Frankfurt' year, the German industry earned a considerable proportion of the headlines in 1981 and collectively ended the year with arguably the strongest product range in its history. In the main, this has been achieved by the refinement of existing designs rather than through a whole rash of new shapes, for the days of frequent change of body styles are gone for ever. The VAG Group, for example, in subtly re-aligning and thereby expanding the marketing base of their Audi and Volkswagen ranges, have concentrated in the main on improving the specification of familiar models, with particular reference to refinement and economy, and are not alone in highlighting the attractions of an economy fifth gear as a means of containing the size of fuel bills.

Interestingly, however, at the lower end of their product range, they have seen fit to replace their former Polo and Derby models (effectively two-box and three-box versions of the same car) with two distinctly different body styles, the Polo now having a vertical rather than sloping rear hatch (does this mark the beginning of a trend away from the conventional hatchback?) and the Derby a significantly larger two-door body. It may well be that in pursuing this policy the company's management have been influenced by the smaller than anticipated sales volume achieved in some markets by the Avant hatchback derivative of the Audi 100 three-box saloon.

No such thoughts, however, concerned General Motors in formulating the structure of their J-Car range, which in Europe carry the Opel and Vauxhall badges in different markets. The choice in this instance is between two-door and four-door saloons and five-door hatchback models, with a wide variety of trim options and two engine sizes. Following the lead established by the Kadett/Astra models, the Ascona/Cavalier marks another stage in the gradual progression of the world's largest car manufacturing group towards front-wheel drive. All the more intriguing, therefore, is the advance news that Ford's replacement for the current Taunus/Cortina range, due towards the end of 1982, will retain the conventional layout of a front-mounted engine driving through a propeller shaft to a rear-mounted final-drive unit.

It may have come as something of a surprise to observers of car styling that BMW's rebodied 5-series saloons are visually so similar to the cars they replace, when in fact there are virtually no interchangeable panels. However, this company, along with its highly respected neighbour, Mercedes-Benz, is always anxious to stress that it does not believe in change simply for its own sake, and such alterations as have been made to these middleweight saloons are for engineering and aerodynamic reasons and have resulted in important gains in efficiency, and consequently also in refinement.

From Mercedes-Benz the most visually evident development has been the introduction of a pair of prestige two-door coupes based on the latest S-series saloons, in succession to the former SLC design, but of at least equal significance has been the programme of economy improvement which has been spread through the remainder of the product range and which incorporates changes to engines, transmissions, ignition and fuel-supply systems. It is also in keeping with the philosophy of this safety-conscious company that the ABS anti-lock braking system has been made available throughout the model range.

Perhaps the most spectacular achievement of the year in the quest for more fuel-efficient large-displacement engines has been the introduction of HE (High Efficiency) versions of the V-12 cylinder Jaguar XJ saloons (and Daimler equivalents) and XJ-S coupe, thanks to the adoption of the ingenious high-compression cylinder-heads developed by Michael May, the Swiss-based research engineer. Not only has this resulted in spectacular improvements in the economy of this previously thirsty engine, but it points to similar collaborative work being carried out by BL and May on other engines, the fruition of which can be expected in the not too distant future.

For BL as a whole, 1981 marked a small but vital step along the path to recovery and financial viability. The Mini Metro enjoyed a level of acceptance in the marketplace beyond initial expectations and this little car had to shoulder much of the burden of achieving corporate sales targets. The other bright spot was the progressing into production of the Triumph Acclaim, the BL version of the Honda Ballade, as a much needed and logical successor to the Dolomite.

This is much more than a stopgap arrangement pending the arrival of BL's LM10 and subsequent models, and there is reason to expect that the BL-Honda tie-up, which offers benefits to both parties, will embrace much more than the existing Acclaim. Just as the Acclaim/Ballade has been improved in both suspension performance and interior packaging as a result of BL's engineering input, future joint models are also likely to reflect the best efforts of both manufacturers at the design and development stages.

Against a backcloth of understandable concern about the level of Japanese car penetration into the US and European markets, there has been a strengthening of ties between manufacturers in Japan and the other major car-producing countries, and there is little doubt that these multi-national arrangements will be a vital part of the long-term health, and in some cases even survival, of the industry. We have yet to see the product of the Italian-based union between Alfa Romeo and Nissan, but its impact will have far-reaching implications for other manufacturers, while in South-East Asia and adjacent territories the Japanese industry so dominates the market that US and European manufacturers have in the main only been able to retain a significant interest there through their equity involvements and the joint manufacturing/marketing arrangements which these have facilitated.

In the longer term, one of the most interesting associations concerns Lotus and Toyota, one outcome of which is expected to be the supply of mechanical units for a future lower-priced Lotus sports car on the one hand, and on the other the supply of Lotus design, research and development expertise to their Japanese partner. Whether the association will also have implications for Lotus in the Grand Prix motor racing field in the future is a matter for some speculation, but if so it would presumably involve a turbocharged engine.

The trend towards turbos continues in the passenger-car field, although the speed of the development in 1980 has understandably slackened somewhat since. However, following Saab's successful integration of their 900 Turbo with automatic transmission their Swedish rivals have entered the forced-induction arena by offering a turbocharged version of their 245 estate car. Renault, meanwhile, are reportedly delighted with the impact of their R18 Turbo saloon, and there is good reason to expect that the French manufacturer will continue to expand their range of turbo-equipped cars during the next year.

In all major markets, 1981 was a year when the industry continued to manufacture some very effective ammunition, but the battle was fought, as always, through the dealerships, and more than ever before it was the quality of the manufacturer/distributor relationship, and the ability and willingness of each to help the other during periods of particular difficulty, which determined the level of success they jointly achieved. There is little doubt that much the same situation will occur throughout 1982, when the quality of the means of distribution, rather than that of the product itself, is likely to be tested the more severely.

INTERNATIONAL REGISTRATION LETTERS

These consist of one, two or three letters of the same size, usually in black, set on a white oval background. They indicate the country of origin as set out below, and are displayed by cars which are being driven in foreign countries.

They have also been used throughout this book to indicate countries of manufacture.

Not all countries subscribe to this system of identification, however. For example, a plate bearing the letters TT (*Titre Temporaire*) shows that the owner has temporarily registered in France, though he may have come from another country originally. The letters following TT indicate the particular district of France where the registration was taken out.

Those plates with prefixes from QA to QS are issued by the R.A.C. or the A.A. in this country to vehicles temporarily imported from abroad. Numbers prefaced by EE indicate a first temporary registration for touring from Italy.

Cars used by High Commissioners in this country carry small plates bearing the letters HC, and those used by Foreign Embassies and Legations have a plate with the letters CD in addition to their registration plates.

The letters given in brackets are proposed new signs which are being or will be introduced. An asterisk denotes a country in which the rule of the road is drive on the left; otherwise drive on the right.

A (AT)	Austria	CL (LK)	Sri Lanka (formerly Ceylon)*
ADN (YD)	Democratic Yemen (formerly Aden)*	CO	Colombia
AFG (AF)	Afghanistan	CR	Costa Rica
AL	Albania	CS	Czechoslovakia
AND (AD)	Andorra	CY	Cyprus*
AUS (AU)	Australia*	D (DE)	German Federal Republic
B (BE)	Belgium	DDR (DD)	German Democratic Republic
BD	Bangladesh		
BDS (BB)	Barbados*	DK	Denmark
BG	Bulgaria	DOM (DO)	Dominican Republic
BH (BZ)	Belize (formerly British Honduras)	DY	Benin (formerly Dahomey)
BR	Brazil		
BRN (BH)	Bahrain	DZ	Algeria
BRU (BN)	Brunei*	E (ES)	Spain (including African territories)
BS	Bahamas*		
BUR (BU)	Burma	EAK (KE)	Kenya*
C (CU)	Cuba	EAT (TZ)	Tanzania (formerly Tanganyika)
CDN (CA)	Canada		
CH	Switzerland	EAU (UG)	Uganda*
CI	Ivory Coast		

11

EAZ (TZ)	Tanzania (formerly Zanzibar)*	NL	Netherlands
EC	Ecuador	NZ	New Zealand*
ES	El Salvador	P (PT)	Portugal
ET (EG)	Arab Republic of Egypt	P (AO)	Angola
		P (CV)	Cape Verde Islands
F (FR)	France (including overseas departments and territories)*	P (MZ)	Mozambique*
		P (GN)	Guinea-Bissau
		P (TP)	Timor
FJI (FJ)	Fiji*	P (ST)	São Tomé and Principe
FL (LI)	Liechtenstein		
FR	Faroe Islands	PA	Panama
GB	United Kingdom of Great Britain and Northern Ireland*	PAK (PK)	Pakistan*
		PE	Peru
		PL	Poland
GBA	Alderney*	PNG	Papua New Guinea
GBG	Guernsey* } Channel Islands	PY	Paraguay
GBJ	Jersey*	R (RO)	Romania
GBM	Isle of Man	RA (AR)	Argentina
GBZ (GI)	Gibraltar	RB (BW)	Botswana (formerly Bechuanaland)*
GCA (GT)	Guatemala	RC (TW)	Taiwan (Republic of China)
GH	Ghana		
GR	Greece	RCA (CF)	Central African Republic
GUY (GY)	Guyana* (formerly British Guiana)	RCB (CG)	Congo
		RCH (CL)	Chile
H (HU)	Hungary	RH (HT)	Haiti
HK	Hong Kong*	RI (ID)	Indonesia*
HKJ (JO)	Jordan	RIM (MR)	Mauritania
I (IT)	Italy	RL (LB)	Lebanon
IL	Israel	RM (MG)	Madagascar
IND (IN)	India*	RMM (ML)	Mali
IR	Iran		
IRL (IE)	Ireland*	RN	Niger
IRQ (IQ)	Iraq	ROK (KP)	Korea (Republic of)
IS	Iceland	RP (PH)	Philippines
J (JP)	Japan*	RSM (SM)	San Marino
JA (JM)	Jamaica*	RSR	Zimbabwe (formerly Rhodesia)*
K (KH)	Kampuchea (Cambodia)		
		RU (BI)	Burundi
KWT (KW)	Kuwait	RWA (RW)	Rwanda
L (LU)	Luxembourg	S (SE)	Sweden
LAO (LA)	Laos	SD (SZ)	Swaziland*
LAR (LY)	Libya	SF (FI)	Finland
LB (LR)	Liberia	SGP (SG)	Singapore*
LS	Lesotho (formerly Basutoland)*	SME (SR)	Surinam (formerly Dutch Guiana)*
M (MT)	Malta*	SN	Senegal
MA	Morocco	SU	Union of Soviet Socialist Republics
MAL (MY)	Malaysia*		
MC	Monaco	SWA	South West Africa*
MEX (MX)	Mexico	SY (SC)	Seychelles*
MS (MU)	Mauritius*	SYR (SY)	Syria
MW	Malawi*	T (TH)	Thailand*
N (NO)	Norway	TG	Togo
NA (AN)	Netherlands Antilles	TN	Tunisia
NIC (NI)	Nicaragua		

TR	Turkey	WS	Western Samoa•
TT	Trinidad and Tobago•	WV (VC)	St Vincent
U (UY)	Uruguay		(Windward Islands)•
USA (US)	United States of America	YU	Yugoslavia
		YV (VE)	Venezuela
V (VA)	Vatican City	Z	Zambia•
VN (VD)	Vietnam (Republic of)	ZA	South Africa•
WAG (GM)	Gambia	ZRE (ZM)	Zaire (formerly Congo Kinshasha)
WAL (SL)	Sierra Leone		
WAN (NG)	Nigeria		
WD (DM)	Dominica• ⎫ Wind-		
WG (GD)	Granada• ⎬ ward		
WL (LC)	St Lucia• ⎭ Islands		

ALFA ROMEO (I)　　Alfasud Hatchback 1.3

Identification: Least powerful model in four-car range of three-door saloons, replacing two-door models and supplementing four-door versions. Also available as 1.5 with 85-bhp engine.

Engine: Front-mounted four-cylinder horizontally opposed with belt-driven overhead camshafts and Solex or Dellorto carburettor. Bore × stroke 80 × 67.2 mm, displacement 1350 cc. Output 58 kW (79 bhp) @ 6000 rpm, torque 111 Nm (80 lb ft) @ 3500 rpm.

Transmission: Single-disc diaphragm clutch and five-speed manual gearbox. Front-wheel drive.

Suspension: Front, independent with MacPherson struts, coil springs, telescopic shock absorbers and anti-roll bar. Rear, dead axle with Watt linkage, Panhard rod, coil springs and telescopic shock absorbers.

Steering: Rack and pinion.

Brakes: Discs front and rear, servo-assisted.

Tyres: 165/70 SR–13.

Dimensions: Length 3978 mm (156.6 in), width 1590 mm (62.6 in), height 1370 mm (53.9 in), wheelbase 2456 mm (96.7 in).

Unladen weight: 895 kg (1973 lb).

Notes: Standard equipment includes luggage compartment cover, fold-flat rear seat, fabric upholstery and floor-mounted rear hatch release.

ALFA ROMEO (I)   Alfasud Hatchback Ti 1.5

Identification: Most powerful model in Alfasud hatchback range, supplementing 1.3, Ti 1.3 and 1.5 models and augmenting four-door saloons.

Engine: Front-mounted four-cylinder horizontally opposed with belt-driven overhead camshafts and two twin-choke Weber carburettors. Bore × stroke 84 × 67.2 mm, displacement 1490 cc. Output 70 kW (95 bhp) @ 5800 rpm, torque 130 Nm (94 lb ft) @ 4000 rpm.

Transmission: Single-disc diaphragm clutch and five-speed manual gearbox. Front-wheel drive.

Suspension: Front, independent with MacPherson struts, coil springs, telescopic shock absorbers and anti-roll bar. Rear, dead axle with Watt linkage, Panhard rod, coil springs and telescopic shock absorbers.

Steering: Rack and pinion.

Brakes: Discs front and rear, servo-assisted.

Tyres: 165/70 SR–13.

Dimensions: Length 3978 mm (156.6 in), width 1616 mm (63.6 in), height 1370 mm (53.9 in), wheelbase 2456 mm (96.7 in).

Unladen weight: 895 kg (1973 lb).

Notes: Standard equipment includes items listed for 1.3 model plus front and rear spoilers, dual halogen headlamps, rear screen wash/wipe and breakerless electronic ignition.

ALFA ROMEO (I)   Alfasud Sprint Veloce 1.5

Identification: Top model in Alfasud range combining three-door coupe bodywork with 1.5-litre engine also used in Ti three-door hatchback saloon.

Engine: Front-mounted four-cylinder horizontally opposed with belt-driven overhead camshafts and two twin-choke Weber carburettors. Bore × stroke 84 × 67.2 mm, displacement 1490 cc. Output 70 kW (95 bhp) @ 5800 rpm, torque 133 Nm (96 lb ft) @ 4000 rpm.

Transmission: Single-disc diaphragm clutch and five-speed manual gearbox. Front-wheel drive.

Suspension: Front, independent with MacPherson struts, coil springs, telescopic shock absorbers and anti-roll bar. Rear, dead axle with Watt linkage, Panhard rod, coil springs and telescopic shock absorbers.

Steering: Rack and pinion.

Brakes: Discs front and rear, servo-assisted.

Tyres: 165/70 SR–13.

Dimensions: Length 4020 mm (158.3 in), width 1610 mm (63.4 in), height 1305 mm (51.4 in), wheelbase 2456 mm (96.7 in).

Unladen weight: 900 kg (1984 lb).

Notes: Standard equipment includes alloy wheels, dual head-lamps, luggage compartment cover, integral front and rear spoilers and fabric upholstery.

ALFA ROMEO (I)   Giulietta 1.6

Identification: Least powerful of three versions of Giulietta saloon, supplementing 1.8 and 2.0-litre models and having slightly simpler mechanical and equipment specification.

Engine: Front-mounted four-cylinder in-line with twin chain-driven overhead camshafts and twin Dellorto or Solex carburettors. Bore × stroke 78 × 82 mm, displacement 1570 cc. Output 82 kW (109 bhp) @ 5600 rpm, torque 145 Nm (105 lb ft) @ 4300 rpm.

Transmission: Single-disc diaphragm clutch and five-speed manual gearbox. Rear-wheel drive.

Suspension: Front, independent with wishbones, torsion bars, telescopic shock absorbers and anti-roll bar. Rear, de Dion axle with trailing arms, Watt linkage, coil springs, telescopic shock absorbers and anti-roll bar.

Steering: Rack and pinion.

Brakes: Discs front and rear, servo-assisted.

Tyres: 165 SR–13.

Dimensions: Length 4210 mm (165.8 in), width 1650 mm (65 in), height 1400 mm (55.1 in), wheelbase 2510 mm (98.8 in).

Unladen weight: 1075 kg (2369 lb).

Notes: Standard equipment includes fabric upholstery, head restraints, adjustable steering wheel, centre console and locking fuel filler cap.

ALFA ROMEO (I)   Alfetta 2.0

Identification: Four-door saloon bridging gap between Giulietta and Alfa 6 models and powered by 2-litre engine also used in Alfetta GTV three-door coupe derivative.

Engine: Front-mounted four-cylinder in-line with twin chain-driven overhead camshafts and twin Dellorto or Solex carburettors. Bore × stroke 84 × 88.5 mm, displacement 1962 cc. Output 97 kW (130 bhp) @ 5400 rpm, torque 180 Nm (130 lb ft) @ 4000 rpm.

Transmission: Single-disc diaphragm clutch and five-speed manual gearbox. Rear-wheel drive.

Suspension: Front, independent with wishbones, torsion bars, telescopic shock absorbers and anti-roll bar. Rear, de Dion axle with trailing arms, Watt linkage, coil springs, telescopic shock absorbers and anti-roll bar.

Steering: Rack and pinion.

Brakes: Discs front and rear, servo-assisted.

Tyres: 185/70 HR–14.

Dimensions: Length 4380 mm (172.4 in), width 1640 mm (64.6 in), height 1430 mm (56.3 in), wheelbase 2510 mm (98.8 in).

Unladen weight: 1090 kg (2403 lb).

Notes: Standard equipment includes fabric upholstery, head restraints, tinted glass, centre console and halogen headlamps.

ALFA ROMEO (I)

Identification: New high-performance coupe combining body-work previously only available with 2-litre four-cylinder engine with V-6 engine also fitted to Alfa 6 saloon in carburettor form.

Engine: Front-mounted V-6-cylinder with belt-driven overhead camshafts and Bosch electronic fuel injection. Bore × stroke 88 × 68.3 mm, displacement 2492 cc. Output 120 kW (160 bhp) @ 6000 rpm, torque 213 Nm (154 lb ft) @ 4000 rpm.

Transmission: Twin-disc diaphragm clutch and five-speed manual gearbox. Rear-wheel drive.

Suspension: Front, independent with wishbones, torsion bars, telescopic shock absorbers and anti-roll bar. Rear, de Dion axle with trailing arms, Watt linkage, coil springs, telescopic shock absorbers and anti-roll bar.

Steering: Rack and pinion.

Brakes: Ventilated discs front, discs rear, servo-assisted.

Tyres: 195/60 HR–15.

Dimensions: Length 4260 mm (167.7 in), width 1664 mm (65.5 in), height 1330 mm (52.4 in), wheelbase 2400 mm (94.5 in).

Unladen weight: 1210 kg (2675 lb).

Notes: Standard equipment includes alloy wheels, front and rear spoilers, electrically operated exterior mirror, dual headlamps and velour upholstery.

ALFA ROMEO (I)   Alfa 6

Identification: Flagship of Alfa Romeo range combining body styling based on Alfetta shape in larger format with six-cylinder engine used in fuel-injected form in GTV coupe.

Engine: Front-mounted V-6-cylinder with belt-driven overhead camshafts and six Dellorto carburettors. Bore × stroke 88 × 68.3 mm, displacement 2492 cc. Output 118 kW (158 bhp) @ 5600 rpm, torque 220 Nm (162 lb ft) @ 4000 rpm.

Transmission: Three-speed automatic transmission. Rear-wheel drive.

Suspension: Front, independent with parallel links, torsion bars, telescopic shock absorbers and anti-roll bar. Rear, de Dion axle with Watt linkage, coil springs, telescopic shock absorbers and anti-roll bar.

Steering: Rack and pinion, power-assisted.

Brakes: Ventilated discs front, discs rear, servo-assisted.

Tyres: 195/70 HR–14.

Dimensions: Length 4760 mm (187.4 in), width 1684 mm (66.3 in), height 1394 mm (54.9 in), wheelbase 2600 mm (102.4 in).

Unladen weight: 1430 kg (3152 lb).

Notes: Standard equipment includes alloy wheels, electric window lifts, central locking, electrically operated driver's seat height adjustment and remote-control door mirrors.

ASTON MARTIN (GB)   V8 Vantage

Identification: Further-refined version of highest-performance model in Aston Martin range incorporating uprated engine and suspension, front and rear spoilers and low-profile wide-based tyres.

Engine: Front-mounted V-8-cylinder with twin chain-driven overhead camshafts per bank and four twin-choke Weber carburettors. Bore × stroke 100 × 85 mm, displacement 5340 cc. Output and torque undisclosed.

Transmission: Single-disc diaphragm clutch and five-speed manual gearbox. Rear-wheel drive.

Suspension: Front, independent with wishbones, coil springs, telescopic shock absorbers and anti-roll bar. Rear, de Dion axle with trailing arms, Watt linkage, coil springs and telescopic shock absorbers.

Steering: Rack and pinion, power-assisted.

Brakes: Ventilated discs front and rear, servo-assisted.

Tyres: 255/60 VR–15.

Dimensions: Length 4667 mm (183.8 in), width 1829 mm (72 in), height 1327 mm (52.2 in), wheelbase 2611 mm (102.8 in).

Unladen weight: 1730 kg (3813 lb).

Notes: Standard equipment includes air-conditioning, PowrLok limited-slip differential, leather upholstery and trim, auxiliary lamps, alloy wheels and passenger's foot rest.

ASTON MARTIN (GB)   Lagonda

Identification: Four-door luxury saloon with advanced styling and comprehensive equipment based on Aston Martin mechanical units and running gear.

Engine: Front-mounted V-8-cylinder with twin chain-driven overhead camshafts per cylinder bank and four twin-choke Weber carburettors. Bore × stroke 100 × 85 mm, displacement 5340 cc. Output and torque undisclosed.

Transmission: Three-speed automatic transmission. Rear-wheel drive.

Suspension: Front, independent with wishbones, coil springs, telescopic shock absorbers and anti-roll bar. Rear, de Dion axle with trailing arms, Watt linkage, coil springs and telescopic shock absorbers. Self-levelling.

Steering: Rack and pinion, power-assisted.

Brakes: Ventilated discs front and rear, servo-assisted.

Tyres: 235/70 HR–15.

Dimensions: Length 5283 mm (208 in), width 1816 mm (71.5 in), height 1302 mm (51.3 in), wheelbase 2915 mm (114.8 in).

Unladen weight: 2064 kg (4550 lb).

Notes: Standard equipment includes air-conditioning, dual halogen headlamps, power-adjustable front seats, electric window lifts, central locking and tinted glass.

AUDI (D) 80 CD

Identification: New top model in Audi 80 saloon range with five-cylinder engine formerly only available in Audi Coupe and supplementing 80 C, CL, GL and GLE models.

Engine: Front-mounted five-cylinder in-line with belt-driven overhead camshaft and twin-choke Solex carburettor. Bore × stroke 79.5 × 77.4 mm, displacement 1921 cc. Output 86 kW (115 bhp) @ 5900 rpm, torque 155 Nm (114 lb ft) @ 3700 rpm.

Transmission: Single-disc diaphragm clutch and five-speed manual gearbox, three-speed automatic transmission optional extra. Front-wheel drive.

Suspension: Front, independent with MacPherson struts, coil springs, telescopic shock absorbers and anti-roll bar. Rear, dead axle with trailing arms, Panhard rod, coil springs and telescopic shock absorbers.

Steering: Rack and pinion.

Brakes: Discs front, drums rear, servo-assisted.

Tyres: 175/70 HR–13.

Dimensions: Length 4383 mm (172.6 in), width 1682 mm (66.2 in), height 1365 mm (53.7 in), wheelbase 2538 mm (99.9 in).

Unladen weight: 1020 kg (2248 lb).

Notes: Standard equipment includes fabric upholstery, head restraints, height-adjustable driver's seat, headlamp washers, front air dam and alloy wheels.

AUDI (D)   Coupe

Identification: Four-seater two-door model combining body-shell first seen on Quattro with Audi 80 floor pan and 1.9-litre version of five-cylinder petrol engine.

Engine: Front-mounted five-cylinder in-line with belt-driven overhead camshaft and Zenith carburettor. Bore × stroke 79.5 × 77.4 mm, displacement 1921 cc. Output 86 kW (115 bhp) @ 5900 rpm, torque 155 Nm (114 lb ft) @ 3700 rpm.

Transmission: Single-disc diaphragm clutch and five-speed manual gearbox, three-speed automatic transmission optional extra. Front-wheel drive.

Suspension: Front, independent with MacPherson struts, coil springs, telescopic shock absorbers and anti-roll bar. Rear, semi-independent with trailing arms, coil springs, Panhard rod, telescopic shock absorbers and anti-roll bar.

Steering: Rack and pinion, power-assistance optional extra.

Brakes: Discs front, drums rear, servo-assisted.

Tyres: 175/70 HR–13.

Dimensions: Length 4348 mm (171.2 in), width 1681 mm (66.2 in), height 1350 mm (53.1 in), wheelbase 2542 mm (100.1 in).

Unladen weight: 1022 kg (2252 lb).

Notes: Standard equipment includes tweed-trimmed upholstery, velour carpeting, tinted glass, front and rear spoilers, alloy wheels, central locking and electric window lifts.

AUDI (D)

Identification: Additional model to re-aligned Audi 100 range combining high level of interior equipment with sporting exterior features and also available with carburettor-equipped 1.6 and 2.2-litre engines.

Engine: Front-mounted five-cylinder in-line with belt-driven overhead camshaft and Bosch K-Jetronic fuel injection. Bore × stroke 79.5 × 86.4 mm, displacement 2144 cc. Output 100 kW (136 bhp) @ 5700 rpm, torque 185 Nm (134 lb ft) @ 4800 rpm.

Transmission: Single-disc diaphragm clutch and four-speed manual gearbox, five-speed manual gearbox or three-speed automatic transmission optional extra. Front-wheel drive.

Suspension: Front, independent with MacPherson struts, coil springs, telescopic shock absorbers and anti-roll bar. Rear, dead axle with trailing arms, coil springs, Panhard rod, telescopic shock absorbers and anti-roll bar.

Steering: Rack and pinion, power-assisted.

Brakes: Discs front, drums rear, servo-assisted.

Tyres: 185–70 HR–14.

Dimensions: Length 4683 mm (184.4 in), width 1768 mm (69.6 in), height 1390 mm (54.7 in), wheelbase 2685 mm (105.7 in).

Unladen weight: 1210 kg (2667 lb).

Notes: Standard equipment includes fabric upholstery, head restraints, alloy wheels, four-spoke steering wheel, front air dam, extended centre console and body side rubbing strips.

AUDI (D)

100 Avant CL 5S

Identification: Intermediate model in range of five-cylinder-engined Avant hatchback saloons, bridging gap between 100-bhp and 136-bhp models and also available in GL and CD trim levels.

Engine: Front-mounted five-cylinder in-line with belt-driven overhead camshaft and Zenith carburettor. Bore × stroke 79.5 × 86.4 mm, displacement 2144 cc. Output 85 kW (115 bhp) @ 5400 rpm, torque 170 Nm (122 lb ft) @ 3400 rpm.

Transmission: Single-disc diaphragm clutch and four-speed manual gearbox, five-speed manual gearbox or three-speed automatic transmission optional extra. Front-wheel drive.

Suspension: Front, independent with MacPherson struts, coil springs, telescopic shock absorbers and anti-roll bar. Rear, dead axle with trailing arms, coil springs, Panhard rod, telescopic shock absorbers and anti-roll bar.

Steering: Rack and pinion, power-assistance optional extra.

Brakes: Discs front, drums rear, servo-assisted.

Tyres: 165 SR–14.

Dimensions: Length 4590 mm (180.7 in), width 1768 mm (69.6 in), height 1390 mm (54.7 in), wheelbase 2685 mm (105.7 in).

Unladen weight: 1170 kg (2579 lb).

Notes: Standard equipment includes fabric upholstery, head restraints, fog lamps, headlamp washers, rear screen wash/wipe and locking fuel filler cover.

AUDI (D)

Identification: Joint flagship of Audi saloon range, supplementing 200 turbocharged version and powered by similar 2.1-litre engine in fuel-injected form.

Engine: Front-mounted five-cylinder in-line with belt-driven overhead camshaft and Bosch K-Jetronic fuel injection. Bore × stroke 79.5 × 86.4 mm, displacement 2144 cc. Output 102 kW (136 bhp) @ 5700 rpm, torque 176 Nm (127 lb ft) @ 4200 rpm.

Transmission: Single-disc diaphragm clutch and five-speed manual gearbox, three-speed automatic transmission optional extra. Front-wheel drive.

Suspension: Front, independent with MacPherson struts, coil springs, telescopic shock absorbers and anti-roll bar. Rear, dead axle with trailing arms, coil springs, Panhard rod, telescopic shock absorbers and anti-roll bar.

Steering: Rack and pinion, power-assisted.

Brakes: Ventilated discs front, discs rear, power-assisted.

Tyres: 205/60 HR–15.

Dimensions: Length 4680 mm (184.3 in), width 1768 mm (69.6 in), height 1393 mm (54.8 in), wheelbase 2677 mm (105.4 in).

Unladen weight: 1260 kg (2777 lb).

Notes: Standard equipment includes stereo radio/cassette player, electrically operated sliding roof and window lifts, central locking, cruise control and alloy wheels.

Identification: High-performance turbocharged four-wheel-drive four-seater coupe based on Audi 80 floor pan and incorporating body structure also used for Audi Coupe.

Engine: Front-mounted five-cylinder in-line with belt-driven overhead camshaft, Bosch K-Jetronic fuel injection and KKK exhaust-driven turbocharger. Bore × stroke 79.5 × 86.4 mm, displacement 2144 cc. Output 150 kW (200 bhp) @ 5500 rpm, torque 285 Nm (210 lb ft) @ 3500 rpm.

Transmission: Single-disc diaphragm clutch and five-speed manual gearbox. Four-wheel drive.

Suspension: Front, independent with MacPherson struts, coil springs, telescopic shock absorbers and anti-roll bar. Rear, independent with trailing links, MacPherson struts, coil springs, telescopic shock absorbers and anti-roll bar.

Steering: Rack and pinion, power-assisted.

Brakes: Ventilated discs front, discs rear, power-assisted.

Tyres: 205/60 VR–15.

Dimensions: Length 4404 mm (173.4 in), width 1723 mm (67.8 in), height 1344 mm (52.9 in), wheelbase 2524 mm (99.4 in).

Unladen weight: 1290 kg (2843 lb).

Notes: Standard equipment includes velour upholstery, electric front window lifts and door mirrors, front and rear spoilers and rear screen wash/wipe.

AUSTIN (GB)

Mini 1000 HL

Identification: Improved version of intermediate of three remaining Mini models, bridging gap between similarly powered Mini City saloon and 1000 HL estate.

Engine: Front and transverse-mounted four-cylinder in-line with pushrod-operated overhead valves and SU carburettor. Bore × stroke 64.6 × 76.2 mm, displacement 998 cc. Output 29 kW (39 bhp) @ 4750 rpm, torque 69 Nm (52 lb ft) @ 2000 rpm.

Transmission: Single-disc diaphragm clutch and four-speed manual gearbox. Front-wheel drive.

Suspension: Front, independent with wishbones, rubber cone springs and telescopic shock absorbers. Rear, independent with trailing arms, rubber cone springs and telescopic shock absorbers.

Steering: Rack and pinion.

Brakes: Drums front and rear.

Tyres: 145 SR-10.

Dimensions: Length 3056 mm (120.3 in), width 1410 mm (55.5 in), height 1346 mm (53 in), wheelbase 2037 mm (80.2 in).

Unladen weight: 615 kg (1355 lb).

Notes: Standard equipment includes fabric upholstery, reclining seats, door mirrors, locking fuel filler cap, door bins and Metro steering wheel.

AUSTIN (GB)

Mini Metro 1.0 HLE

Identification: Intermediate model in Metro range combining economical 1-litre engine and high gearing with higher level of trim and equipment than base and L models.

Engine: Front and transverse-mounted four-cylinder in-line with pushrod-operated overhead valves and SU carburettor. Bore × stroke 64.6 × 76.2 mm, displacement 998 cc. Output 34 kW (46 bhp) @ 5500 rpm, torque 75 Nm (54 lb ft) @ 3300 rpm.

Transmission: Single-disc diaphragm clutch and four-speed manual gearbox. Front-wheel drive.

Suspension: Front, independent with transverse links, Hydragas units, telescopic shock absorbers and anti-roll bar. Rear, independent with trailing arms, Hydragas units with integral coil springs and shock absorbers and transverse links.

Steering: Rack and pinion.

Brakes: Discs front, drums rear.

Tyres: 135 SR–12.

Dimensions: Length 3405 mm (134.1 in), width 1549 mm (60.9 in), height 1361 mm (53.6 in), wheelbase 2251 mm (88.6 in).

Unladen weight: 757 kg (1668 lb).

Notes: Standard equipment includes fabric upholstery, rear screen wash/wipe, radio, clock, halogen headlamps and asymmetrically split rear seat.

AUSTIN (GB)   Mini Metro 1.3 Automatic

Identification: Additional model at top end of Metro range combining two-pedal control by uprated AP transmission with high level of equipment.

Engine: Front and transverse-mounted four-cylinder in-line with pushrod-operated overhead valves and SU carburettor. Bore × stroke 70.6 × 81.3 mm, displacement 1275 cc. Output 45 kW (60 bhp) @ 5250 rpm, torque 95 Nm (69 lb ft) @ 3200 rpm.

Transmission: Four-speed automatic transmission. Front-wheel drive.

Suspension: Front, independent with transverse links, Hydragas units, telescopic shock absorbers and anti-roll bar. Rear, independent with trailing arms, Hydragas units with integral coil springs and shock absorbers and transverse links.

Steering: Rack and pinion.

Brakes: Discs front, drums rear, servo-assisted.

Tyres: 155/70 SR–12.

Dimensions: Length 3405 mm (134.1 in), width 1549 mm (60.9 in), height 1361 mm (53.6 in), wheelbase 2251 mm (88.6 in).

Unladen weight: 801 kg (1766 lb).

Notes: Standard equipment includes radio, clock, velour upholstery, reclining front seats with head restraints, asymmetric-split folding rear seat, rear wash/wipe, halogen headlamps and transmission oil cooler.

AUSTIN (GB)

Allegro 1.0 L

Identification: Replacement model at lower end of Allegro range incorporating A-Plus engine from Mini Metro and available in choice of two-door and four-door body styles.

Engine: Front and transverse-mounted four-cylinder in-line with pushrod-operated overhead valves and SU carburettor. Bore × stroke 64.6 × 76.2 mm, displacement 998 cc. Output 33 kW (44 bhp) @ 5250 rpm, torque 72 Nm (52 lb ft) @ 3000 rpm.

Transmission: Single-disc diaphragm clutch and four-speed manual gearbox. Front-wheel drive.

Suspension: Front, independent with wishbones, Hydragas spring units with integral shock absorbers. Rear, independent with trailing arms, Hydragas spring units (linked to front units) with integral shock absorbers.

Steering: Rack and pinion.

Brakes: Discs front, drums rear.

Tyres: 145 SR–13.

Dimensions: Length 3908 mm (153.9 in), width 1613 mm (63.5 in), height 1393 mm (54.8 in), wheelbase 2442 mm (96.1 in).

Unladen weight: 834 kg (1838 lb).

Notes: Standard equipment includes door mirrors, fabric upholstery, wheel trims, reclining seats and body side protection strips.

AUSTIN (GB)

Allegro 1.3 HLS

Identification: Intermediate model in revised Allegro range encompassing 1.0, 1.3, 1.5 and 1.7-litre engines and choice of L, HL and HLS trim levels.

Engine: Front and transverse-mounted four-cylinder in-line with pushrod-operated overhead valves and SU carburettor. Bore × stroke 70.6 × 81.3 mm, displacement 1275 cc. Output 47 kW (63 bhp) @ 5600 rpm, torque 101 Nm (73 lb ft) @ 3200 rpm.

Transmission: Single-disc diaphragm clutch and four-speed manual gearbox. Front-wheel drive.

Suspension: Front, independent with wishbones, Hydragas spring units with integral shock absorbers. Rear, independent with trailing arms, Hydragas spring units (linked to front units) with integral shock absorbers.

Steering: Rack and pinion.

Brakes: Discs front, drums rear, servo-assisted.

Tyres: 155 SR–13.

Dimensions: Length 3908 mm (153.9 in), width 1613 mm (63.5 in), height 1393 mm (54.8 in), wheelbase 2442 mm (96.1 in).

Unladen weight: 842 kg (1856 lb).

Notes: Standard equipment includes dual headlamps, radio, door mirrors, tinted glass, velour upholstery, head restraints and locking fuel filler cap.

BENTLEY (GB)

Mulsanne

Identification: Bentley equivalent of Rolls-Royce Silver Spirit saloon, replacing T2 four-door model and incorporating suspension derived from Corniche convertible.

Engine: Front-mounted V-8-cylinder with pushrod-operated overhead valves and twin SU carburettors. Bore × stroke 104.1 × 99.1 mm, displacement 6750 cc. Output and torque undisclosed.

Transmission: Three-speed automatic transmission. Rear-wheel drive.

Suspension: Front, independent with wishbones, coil springs, telescopic shock absorbers and anti-roll bar. Rear, independent with trailing arms, coil springs, auxiliary gas springs, strut-type shock absorbers and anti-roll bar. Self-levelling.

Steering: Rack and pinion, power-assisted.

Brakes: Ventilated discs front, discs rear, power-assisted.

Tyres: 235/70 HR–15.

Dimensions: Length 5309 mm (209 in), width 1887 mm (74.3 in), height 1485 mm (58.5 in), wheelbase 3061 mm (120.5 in).

Unladen weight: 2245 kg (4948 lb).

Notes: Standard equipment includes air-conditioning, headlamp wash/wipe, electrically operated gear selection, front seat adjustment, windows, mirrors, central locking fuel-filler cap and aerial and stereo radio/cassette player with four speakers.

BMW (D)

Identification: Smallest-engined model in BMW 3-series range with five-speed transmission aimed at further reduction in fuel consumption and augmenting similarly bodied 320 and 323i models.

Engine: Front-mounted four-cylinder in-line with belt-driven overhead camshaft and Solex carburettor. Bore × stroke 89 × 71 mm, displacement 1766 cc. Output 67 kW (90 bhp) @ 5500 rpm, torque 142 Nm (105 lb ft) @ 3500 rpm.

Transmission: Single-disc diaphragm clutch and five-speed manual gearbox. Rear-wheel drive.

Suspension: Front, independent with MacPherson struts, coil springs, telescopic shock absorbers and anti-roll bar. Rear, independent with trailing arms, coil springs and telescopic shock absorbers.

Steering: Rack and pinion.

Brakes: Discs front, drums rear, servo-assisted.

Tyres: 165 SR-13.

Dimensions: Length 4350 mm (171.3 in), width 1610 mm (63.4 in), height 1380 mm (54.3 in), wheelbase 2563 mm (101 in).

Unladen weight: 1020 kg (2249 lb).

Notes: Standard equipment includes fabric upholstery, halogen headlamps, transistorized ignition, head restraints and electrically operated door mirrors.

BMW (D) **323i**

Identification: High-performance model at top end of range of 3-series two-door saloons, supplementing 316, 318 and 320 models.

Engine: Front-mounted six-cylinder in-line with belt-driven overhead camshaft and Bosch K-Jetronic fuel injection. Bore × stroke 80 × 76.8 mm, displacement 2315 cc. Output 105 kW (143 bhp) @ 6000 rpm, torque 190 Nm (140 lb ft) @ 4500 rpm.

Transmission: Single-disc diaphragm clutch and five-speed manual gearbox. Rear-wheel drive.

Suspension: Front, independent with MacPherson struts, coil springs, telescopic shock absorbers and anti-roll bar. Rear, independent with trailing arms, coil springs and telescopic shock absorbers.

Steering: Rack and pinion, power assistance optional extra.

Brakes: Discs front, drums rear, servo-assisted.

Tyres: 185/70 HR–13.

Dimensions: Length 4350 mm (171.3 in), width 1610 mm (63.4 in), height 1380 mm (54.3 in), wheelbase 2563 mm (101 in).

Unladen weight: 1135 kg (2502 lb).

Notes: Standard equipment includes velour upholstery, dual halogen headlamps, head restraints and body side mouldings.

BMW (D)   520i

Identification: Smallest six-cylinder-engined model in revised range of 5-series saloons, bridging gap between four-cylinder 518 and six-cylinder 525i versions.

Engine: Front-mounted six-cylinder in-line with belt-driven overhead camshaft and Bosch K-Jetronic fuel injection. Bore × stroke 66 × 80 mm, displacement 1990 cc. Output 94 kW (125 bhp) @ 5800 rpm, torque 167 Nm (121 lb ft) @ 4500 rpm.

Transmission: Single-disc diaphragm clutch and four-speed manual gearbox, five-speed manual gearbox or three-speed automatic transmission optional extra. Rear-wheel drive.

Suspension: Front, independent with MacPherson struts, coil springs, telescopic shock absorbers and anti-roll bar. Rear, independent with trailing arms, coil springs and telescopic shock absorbers.

Steering: Worm and roller, power-assisted.

Brakes: Discs front, drums rear, servo-assisted.

Tyres: 175 HR-14.

Dimensions: Length 4620 mm (181.9 in), width 1700 mm (66.9 in), height 1415 mm (55.7 in), wheelbase 2625 mm (103.3 in).

Unladen weight: 1218 kg (2686 lb).

Notes: Standard equipment includes revised instrumentation incorporating service interval indicator, electronic temperature control, dual halogen headlamps and fabric upholstery.

BMW (D)   528i

Identification: Top model in four-car range of latest 5-series saloons incorporating revised rear suspension and supplementing 518, 520i and 525i models.

Engine: Front-mounted six-cylinder in-line with chain-driven overhead camshaft and Bosch L-Jetronic fuel injection. Bore × stroke 80 × 86 mm, displacement 2788 cc. Output 138 kW (184 bhp) @ 5800 rpm, torque 245 Nm (177 lb ft) @ 4200 rpm.

Transmission: Single-disc diaphragm clutch and five-speed manual gearbox, three-speed automatic transmission optional extra. Rear-wheel drive.

Suspension: Front, independent with MacPherson struts, coil springs, telescopic shock absorbers and anti-roll bar. Rear, independent with trailing arms and additional links, coil springs, telescopic shock absorbers and anti-roll bar.

Steering: Worm and roller, power-assisted.

Brakes: Ventilated discs front, discs rear, power-assisted.

Tyres: 195/70 VR–14.

Dimensions: Length 4620 mm (181.9 in), width 1700 mm (66.9 in), height 1415 mm (55.7 in), wheelbase 2625 mm (103.3 in).

Unladen weight: 1319 kg (2907 lb).

Notes: Standard equipment includes revised instrumentation incorporating service interval indicator, fuel consumption meter and overhead warning light display, velour upholstery and alloy wheels.

BMW (D)

Identification: Smaller-engined of two 6-series two-door four-seater coupes, supplementing 635 CSi and powered by similar engine to that used in 728i saloon.

Engine: Front-mounted six-cylinder in-line with chain-driven overhead camshaft and Bosch L-Jetronic fuel injection. Bore × stroke 86 × 80 mm, displacement 2788 cc. Output 138 kW (184 bhp) @ 5800 rpm, torque 245 Nm (177 lb ft) @ 4200 rpm.

Transmission: Single-disc diaphragm clutch and five-speed manual gearbox, three-speed automatic transmission optional extra. Rear-wheel drive.

Suspension: Front, independent with MacPherson struts, coil springs, telescopic shock absorbers and anti-roll bar. Rear, independent with trailing arms, coil springs and telescopic shock absorbers.

Steering: Worm and roller, power-assisted.

Brakes: Ventilated discs front, discs rear, servo-assisted.

Tyres: 195/70 VR–14.

Dimensions: Length 4750 mm (187 in), width 1720 mm (67.7 in), height 1360 mm (53.5 in), wheelbase 2620 mm (103.2 in).

Unladen weight: 1450 kg (3196 lb).

Notes: Standard equipment includes alloy wheels, velour or leather upholstery, electric window lifts, central locking, tinted glass and height-adjustable seats and steering wheel.

BMW (D) 735i

Identification: Flagship of BMW range in UK and other markets where turbocharged 745i is unobtainable, supplementing 728i and 732i saloons.

Engine: Front-mounted six-cylinder in-line with chain-driven overhead camshaft and Bosch L-Jetronic fuel injection. Bore × stroke 93.4 × 84 mm, displacement 3453 cc. Output 163 kW (218 bhp) @ 5200 rpm, torque 315 Nm (218 lb ft) @ 4000 rpm.

Transmission: Single-disc diaphragm clutch and five-speed manual gearbox, three-speed automatic transmission optional extra. Rear-wheel drive.

Suspension: Front, independent with MacPherson struts, coil springs, telescopic shock absorbers and anti-roll bar. Rear, independent with trailing arms, coil springs and telescopic shock absorbers.

Steering: Recirculating ball, power-assisted.

Brakes: Ventilated discs front, discs rear, servo-assisted.

Tyres: 205/70 VR–14.

Dimensions: Length 4860 mm (191.3 in), width 1800 mm (70.9 in), height 1430 mm (56.3 in), wheelbase 2795 mm (110 in).

Unladen weight: 1530 kg (3372 lb).

Notes: Standard equipment includes alloy wheels, headlamp wash/wipe, carpeted and illuminated luggage compartment, fabric upholstery, front and rear head restraints, central locking and electric window lifts.

BRISTOL (GB)   412/S3 Beaufighter

Identification: Four-seater fixed-head or convertible coupe developed from 412/S2 and incorporating turbocharged engine and restyled upper bodywork with removable glass roof panel as well as dual headlamps.

Engine: Front-mounted V-8-cylinder with pushrod-operated overhead valves, exhaust-driven turbocharger and Carter carburettor. Bore × stroke 101.6 × 90.9 mm, displacement 5900 cc. Output and torque undisclosed.

Transmission: Three-speed automatic transmission. Rear-wheel drive.

Suspension: Front, independent with wishbones, coil springs, adjustable telescopic shock absorbers and anti-roll bar. Rear, live axle with Watt linkage, torsion bars and adjustable telescopic shock absorbers.

Steering: Recirculating ball, power-assisted.

Brakes: Discs front and rear, servo-assisted.

Tyres: 225/70 VR–15.

Dimensions: Length 4940 mm (194.5 in), width 1765 mm (69.5 in), height 1435 mm (56.5 in), wheelbase 2896 mm (114 in).

Unladen weight: 1760 kg (3880 lb).

Notes: Standard equipment includes electrically adjustable seats, removable rear roof section on hardtop version, leather upholstery and automatic door locking.

CITROEN (F)

Identification: Latest version of versatile four-door economy saloon with detail trim improvements and uprated technical specification including disc front brakes.

Engine: Front-mounted two-cylinder horizontally opposed air-cooled with pushrod-operated overhead valves and Solex carburettor. Bore × stroke 74 × 70 mm, displacement 602 cc. Output 22 kW (29 bhp) @ 5750 rpm, torque 40 Nm (29 lb ft) @ 3500 rpm.

Transmission: Single-disc diaphragm clutch and four-speed manual gearbox. Front-wheel drive.

Suspension: Front, independent with leading arms, coil springs and telescopic shock absorbers. Rear, independent with trailing arms, coil springs and telescopic shock absorbers. Suspension arms linked front-to-rear.

Steering: Rack and pinion.

Brakes: Discs front, drums rear.

Tyres: 125–15.

Dimensions: Length 3320 mm (130.7 in), width 1480 mm (58.3 in), height 1600 mm (63 in), wheelbase 2400 mm (94.5 in).

Unladen weight: 560 kg (1235 lb).

Notes: Standard equipment includes fabric upholstery, anti-theft lock, removable rear seat, laminated screen, internally adjustable headlamps and fold-back roof.

CITROEN (F)   Visa II Club

Identification: Higher-specification model of two 652-cc-engined saloons in revised Visa II range, augmenting more powerful models with choice of 1.1-litre and 1.2-litre engines.

Engine: Front-mounted twin-cylinder horizontally opposed air-cooled with pushrod-operated overhead valves and Solex carburettor. Bore × stroke 77 × 70 mm, displacement 652 cc. Output 26 kW (35 bhp) @ 5250 rpm, torque 50 Nm (36 lb ft) @ 3500 rpm.

Transmission: Single-disc diaphragm clutch and four-speed manual gearbox. Front-wheel drive.

Suspension: Front, independent with MacPherson struts, coil springs, telescopic shock absorbers and anti-roll bar. Rear, independent with trailing arms, coil springs and telescopic shock absorbers.

Steering: Rack and pinion.

Brakes: Discs front, drums rear.

Tyres: 135 SR–13.

Dimensions: Length 3690 mm (145.3 in), width 1510 mm (59.5 in), height 1415 mm (55.7 in), wheelbase 2430 mm (95.7 in).

Unladen weight: 745 kg (1642 lb).

Notes: Standard equipment includes folding rear seats, internally adjustable headlamps, heated rear screen, rear screen wash/wipe, reclining front seats, removable rear parcel shelf and quartz clock.

CITROEN (F)   Visa II Super E

Identification: Intermediate model in Visa II range bridging gap between 652-cc-engined Special and Club and 1.2-litre Super X saloons.

Engine: Front and transverse-mounted four-cylinder in-line with chain-driven overhead camshaft and Solex carburettor. Bore × stroke 72 × 69 mm, displacement 1124 cc. Output 37 kW (50 bhp) @ 5500 rpm, torque 84 Nm (61 lb ft) @ 2500 rpm.

Transmission: Single-disc diaphragm clutch and four-speed manual gearbox. Front-wheel drive.

Suspension: Front, independent with MacPherson struts, coil springs, telescopic shock absorbers and anti-roll bar. Rear, independent with trailing arms, coil springs and telescopic shock absorbers.

Steering: Rack and pinion.

Brakes: Discs front, drums rear, servo-assisted.

Tyres: 145 SR–13.

Dimensions: Length 3690 mm (145.3 in), width 1524 mm (60 in), height 1415 mm (55.7 in), wheelbase 2420 mm (95.3 in).

Unladen weight: 810 kg (1786 lb).

Notes: Standard equipment includes halogen headlamps, cigar lighter, econoscope, engine diagnostic socket and all items listed for Visa II Club.

CITROEN (F)

Visa II Super X

Identification: Most powerful model in Visa II range, augmenting 652-cc-engined Special and Club and 1124-cc-engined Super E (economy) models.

Engine: Front and transverse-mounted four-cylinder in-line with chain-driven overhead camshaft and Solex carburettor. Bore × stroke 75 × 69 mm, displacement 1219 cc. Output 48 kW (64 bhp) @ 6000 rpm, torque 93 Nm (67 lb ft) @ 3000 rpm.

Transmission: Single-disc diaphragm clutch and four-speed manual gearbox. Front-wheel drive.

Suspension: Front, independent with MacPherson struts, coil springs, telescopic shock absorbers and anti-roll bar. Rear independent with trailing arms, coil springs and telescopic shock absorbers.

Steering: Rack and pinion.

Brakes: Discs front, drums rear, servo-assisted.

Tyres: 160/65 R340.

Dimensions: Length 3690 mm (145.3 in), width 1524 mm (60 in), height 1397 mm (55 in), wheelbase 2425 mm (95.5 in).

Unladen weight: 815 kg (1797 lb).

Notes: Standard equipment includes alloy wheels, rev counter and all items listed for Super E except econoscope.

CITROEN (F)   GSA Special

Identification: Larger-engined version of model previously only available with 1129-cc engine and supplementing Club and Pallas five-door hatchback saloons.

Engine: Front-mounted four-cylinder horizontally opposed air-cooled with belt-driven overhead camshafts and Weber carburettor. Bore × stroke 79.4 × 65.6 mm, displacement 1299 cc. Output 48 kW (65 bhp) @ 5500 rpm, torque 101 Nm (72 lb ft) @ 3500 rpm.

Transmission: Single-disc diaphragm clutch and four-speed manual gearbox. Front-wheel drive.

Suspension: Front, independent with wishbones, hydropneumatic units and anti-roll bar. Rear, independent with trailing arms, hydropneumatic units and anti-roll bar. Self-levelling front and rear.

Steering: Rack and pinion.

Brakes: Discs front and rear, power-assisted.

Tyres: 145 SR–15.

Dimensions: Length 4195 mm (165·2 in), width 1626 mm (64 in), height 1349 mm (53.1 in), wheelbase 2550 mm (100·4 in).

Unladen weight: 955 kg (2105 lb).

Notes: Standard equipment includes folding rear seat, fabric upholstery, reclining front seats, halogen headlamps, radio aerial and twin speakers and luggage compartment light.

CITROEN (F)

GSA Special Estate

Identification: Five-door estate model in GSA range powered by 1.3-litre engine formerly available in GSA Club models.

Engine: Front-mounted air-cooled four-cylinder horizontally opposed with belt-driven overhead camshafts and Weber carburettor. Bore × stroke 79.4 × 65.6 mm, displacement 1299 cc. Output 48 kW (65 bhp) @ 5500 rpm, torque 101 Nm (72 lb ft) @ 3500 rpm.

Transmission: Single-disc diaphragm clutch and five-speed manual gearbox, three-speed semi-automatic transmission optional extra. Front-wheel drive.

Suspension: Front, independent with wishbones, hydropneumatic units and anti-roll bar. Rear, independent with trailing arms, hydropneumatic units and anti-roll bar. Self-levelling front and rear.

Steering: Rack and pinion.

Brakes: Discs front and rear, power-assisted.

Tyres: 145 SR–15.

Dimensions: Length 4156 mm (163.6 in), width 1626 mm (64 in), height 1349 mm (53.1 in), wheelbase 2550 mm (100.4 in).

Unladen weight: 965 kg (2127 lb).

Notes: Standard equipment includes rear screen wash/wipe, fabric upholstery, clock, load-compensating headlamps and radio aerial and speakers.

CITROEN (F)   CX Reflex Safari

Identification: Smallest-engined estate car in CX range, supplementing 2.4-litre with automatic transmission and 2.5-litre diesel with five-speed manual gearbox.

Engine: Front and transverse-mounted four-cylinder in-line with belt-driven overhead camshaft and Weber carburettor. Bore × stroke 88 × 82 mm, displacement 1995 cc. Output 80 kW (106 bhp) @ 5500 rpm, torque 169 Nm (122 lb ft) @ 3250 rpm.

Transmission: Single-disc diaphragm clutch and five-speed manual gearbox. Front-wheel drive.

Suspension: Front, independent with wishbones, hydropneumatic units and anti-roll bar. Rear, independent with trailing arms, hydropneumatic units and anti-roll bar. Self-levelling front and rear.

Steering: Rack and pinion, power-assisted.

Brakes: Discs front and rear, power-assisted.

Tyres: 185 SR–14.

Dimensions: Length 4953 mm (195 in), width 1734 mm (68.3 in), height 1460 mm (57.5 in), wheelbase 3100 mm (122 in).

Unladen weight: 1260 kg (2777 lb).

Notes: Standard equipment includes rear screen wash/wipe, fabric upholstery, height-adjustable driver's seat, tinted glass, electric window lifts, automatically adjustable headlamps and laminated screen.

CITROEN (F) CX 2400 Pallas Injection Auto

Identification: High-specification CX 2400 saloon, bridging gap between Super and Prestige models and equipped with fully automatic transmission previously only available on Prestige model.

Engine: Front and transverse-mounted four-cylinder in-line with pushrod-operated overhead valves and Bosch L-Jetronic fuel injection. Bore × stroke 93.5 × 85.5 mm, displacement 2347 cc. Output 96 kW (128 bhp) @ 4800 rpm, torque 201 Nm (145 lb ft) @ 3600 rpm.

Transmission: Three-speed automatic transmission or single-disc diaphragm clutch and five-speed manual gearbox. Front-wheel drive.

Suspension: Front, independent with wishbones, hydropneumatic units and anti-roll bar. Rear, independent with trailing arms, hydropneumatic units and anti-roll bar. Self-levelling front and rear.

Steering: Rack and pinion, power-assisted.

Brakes: Discs front and rear, power-assisted.

Tyres: 185 HR–14.

Dimensions: Length 4623 mm (182 in), width 1735 mm (68.3 in), height 1397 mm (55 in), wheelbase 2845 mm (112 in).

Unladen weight: 1370 kg (3020 lb).

Notes: Standard equipment includes central locking, electric front window lifts, tinted glass, height-adjustable driver's seat, radio aerial and speakers and halogen headlamps.

COLT (J)   1200 GL Hatchback

Identification: Additional model in Colt hatchback range, supplementing 1.4-litre-engined GLX three-door and five-door models.

Engine: Front-mounted four-cylinder in-line with belt-driven overhead camshaft and Aisan carburettor. Bore × stroke 59.5 × 82 mm, displacement 1244 cc. Output 41 kW (55 bhp) @ 5000 rpm, torque 91 Nm (66 lb ft) @ 3500 rpm.

Transmission: Single-disc diaphragm clutch and four-speed manual gearbox. Front-wheel drive.

Suspension: Front, independent with MacPherson struts, coil springs, telescopic shock absorbers and anti-roll bar. Rear, independent with trailing arms, coil springs and telescopic shock absorbers.

Steering: Rack and pinion.

Brakes: Discs front, drums rear, servo-assisted.

Tyres: 155 SR–13.

Dimensions: Length 3790 mm (149.2 in), width 1585 mm (62.4 in), height 1345 mm (52.9 in), wheelbase 2300 mm (90.6 in).

Unladen weight: 805 kg (1774 lb).

Notes: Standard equipment includes reclining seats, folding rear seat, radio, halogen headlamps, front and rear stoneguards and rear screen wash/wipe.

COLT (J)   Lancer 1400 GLX

Identification: Improved version of smaller-engined Lancer four-door saloon with uprated transmission and supplementing 1.6-litre-engined GSR version.

Engine: Front-mounted four-cylinder in-line with belt-driven overhead camshaft and Solex carburettor. Bore × stroke 74 × 82 mm, displacement 1410 cc. Output 50 kW (68 bhp) @ 5000 rpm, torque 105 Nm (75 lb ft) @ 3500 rpm.

Transmission: Single-disc diaphragm clutch and five-speed manual gearbox, three-speed automatic transmission optional extra. Rear-wheel drive.

Suspension: Front, independent with MacPherson struts, coil springs, telescopic shock absorbers and anti-roll bar. Rear, live axle with four links, coil springs, telescopic shock absorbers and anti-roll bar.

Steering: Recirculating ball.

Brakes: Discs front, drums rear, servo-assisted.

Tyres: 155 SR–13.

Dimensions: Length 4225 mm (166.3 in), width 1620 mm (63.8 in), height 1385 mm (54.5 in), wheelbase 2440 mm (88.2 in).

Unladen weight: 935 kg (2061 lb).

Notes: Standard equipment includes halogen headlamps, adjustable steering column, radio, transistorized ignition and fabric upholstery.

Identification: Improved version of five-door estate car incorporating new radiator grille and headlamps, increased interior space and revised steering.

Engine: Front-mounted four-cylinder in-line with belt-driven overhead camshaft and Solex carburettor. Bore × stroke 76.9 × 86 mm, displacement 1597 cc. Output 55 kW (74 bhp) @ 5000 rpm, torque 116 Nm (84 lb ft) @ 3000 rpm.

Transmission: Single-disc diaphragm clutch and four-speed manual gearbox. Rear-wheel drive.

Suspension: Front, independent with MacPherson struts, coil springs, telescopic shock absorbers and anti-roll bar. Rear, live axle with four links, coil springs, telescopic shock absorbers and anti-roll bar.

Steering: Recirculating ball.

Brakes: Discs front, drums rear, servo-assisted.

Tyres: 165 SR–14.

Dimensions: Length 4420 mm (174.1 in), width 1670 mm (65.8 in), height 1380 mm (54.4 in), wheelbase 2515 mm (99 in).

Unladen weight: 1075 kg (2370 lb).

Notes: Standard equipment includes height-adjustable steering, carpeted cargo area with automatic light, rear screen wash/wipe, radio, head restraints, tinted glass and halogen headlamps.

COLT (J)   Lancer 2000 Turbo

Identification: Top model in range of four-door saloons featuring turbocharged and fuel-injected 2-litre engine, front and rear spoilers and alloy wheels.

Engine: Front-mounted four-cylinder in-line with belt-driven overhead camshaft, exhaust-driven turbocharger and electronic fuel injection. Bore × stroke 85 × 88 mm, displacement 1997 cc. Output 125 kW (170 bhp) @ 5500 rpm, torque 245 Nm (177 lb ft) @ 3500 rpm.

Transmission: Single-disc diaphragm clutch and five-speed manual gearbox. Rear-wheel drive.

Suspension: Front, independent with MacPherson struts, coil springs, telescopic shock absorbers and anti-roll bar. Rear, live axle with four links, coil springs, telescopic shock absorbers and anti-roll bar.

Steering: Recirculating ball.

Brakes: Ventilated discs front and rear, servo-assisted.

Tyres: 175/70 HR–14.

Dimensions: Length 4225 mm (166.3 in), width 1620 mm (63.8 in), height 1390 mm (54.7 in), wheelbase 2440 mm (88.2 in).

Unladen weight: 1075 kg (2370 lb).

Notes: Standard equipment includes alloy wheels, special paint finish, quartz digital clock, adjustable steering column, halogen headlamps and three-speed wash/wipe system.

COLT (J)   Galant 2000 GLS

Identification: Top model in latest range of four-door saloons incorporating new 2-litre engine with balancer shafts and high level of standard equipment; 1.6-litre version available without independent rear suspension.

Engine: Front-mounted four-cylinder in-line with belt-driven overhead camshaft and Mikuni-Solex carburettor. Bore × stroke 85 × 88 mm, displacement 1997 cc. Output 76 kW (102 bhp) @ 5500 rpm, torque 155 Nm (112 lb ft) @ 3500 rpm.

Transmission: Single-disc diaphragm clutch and five-speed manual gearbox, three-speed automatic transmission optional extra. Rear-wheel drive.

Suspension: Front, independent with MacPherson struts, coil springs, telescopic shock absorbers and anti-roll bar. Rear, independent with trailing arms, coil springs and telescopic shock absorbers.

Steering: Recirculating ball, power-assisted.

Brakes: Discs front and rear, servo-assisted.

Tyres: 165 SR–14.

Dimensions: Length 4470 mm (176 in), width 1680 mm (66.1 in), height 1370 mm (53.9 in), wheelbase 2530 mm (99.6 in).

Unladen weight: 1170 kg (2579 lb).

Notes: Standard equipment includes alloy wheels, electric window lifts, stereo radio/cassette player, headlamp wash/wipe, locking fuel filler cover and height-adjustable driver's seat and steering wheel.

DAIMLER (GB)   Vanden Plas 4.2

Identification: Smaller-engined of two top-specification four-door saloons, supplementing V-12-engined Double Six version and incorporating uprated equipment to widen gap from equivalent Jaguar model.

Engine: Front-mounted six-cylinder in-line with twin chain-driven overhead camshafts and Lucas electronic fuel injection. Bore × stroke 92 × 106 mm, displacement 4235 cc. Output 153 kW (205 bhp) @ 5000 rpm, torque 326 Nm (236 lb ft) @ 3750 rpm.

Transmission: Three-speed automatic transmission. Rear-wheel drive.

Suspension: Front, independent with wishbones, coil springs, telescopic shock absorbers and anti-roll bar. Rear, independent with trailing arms, wishbones, fixed-length drive-shafts, dual coil springs and telescopic shock absorbers.

Steering: Rack and pinion, power-assisted.

Brakes: Ventilated discs front, discs rear, servo-assisted.

Tyres: 205/70 VR–15

Dimensions: Length 4959 mm (195.2 in), width 1770 mm (69.7 in), height 1377 mm (54 in), wheelbase 2865 mm (112.8 in).

Unladen weight: 1832 kg (4040 lb).

Notes: Standard equipment includes cruise control, automatic air-conditioning, distinctive-style hide upholstery, electrically operated front seats and rear-view mirrors and front-to-rear centre console.

DAIMLER (GB)   Double-Six HE

Identification: Intermediate model in Daimler saloon range, bridging gap between six-cylinder XK-engined Sovereign and Vanden Plas models and V-12-engined Vanden Plas.

Engine: Front-mounted V-12-cylinder with single chain-driven overhead camshafts and Lucas electronic digital fuel injection. Bore × stroke 90 × 70 mm, displacement 5343 cc. Output 224 kW (299 bhp) @ 5500 rpm, torque 440 Nm (318 lb ft) @ 3000 rpm.

Transmission: Three-speed automatic transmission. Rear-wheel drive.

Suspension: Front, independent with wishbones, coil springs, telescopic shock absorbers and anti-roll bar. Rear, independent with trailing arms, wishbones, fixed-length drive-shafts, dual coil springs and telescopic shock absorbers.

Steering: Rack and pinion, power-assisted.

Brakes: Ventilated discs front, discs rear, servo-assisted.

Tyres: 215/70 VR–15.

Dimensions: Length 4959 mm (195.2 in), width 1770 mm (69.7 in), height 1377 mm (54 in), wheelbase 2865 mm (112.8 in).

Unladen weight: 1930 kg (4250 lb).

Notes: Standard equipment includes burr walnut dashboard panel and door fillets, front-to-rear centre console, electrically operated front seats, steel sliding roof, rear-view mirrors and headlamp wash/wipe.

DATSUN (J)

Cherry 1.2 GL 3-door Hatchback

Identification: Latest version of Cherry with restyled front end and improved interior specification, also available with five-door bodywork or as three-door L with choice of 1.0 and 1.2-litre engines.

Engine: Front and transverse-mounted four-cylinder in-line with pushrod-operated overhead valves and Hitachi carburettor. Bore × stroke 73 × 70 mm, displacement 1171 cc. Output 38 kW (52 bhp) @ 5600 rpm, torque 80 Nm (57 lb ft) @ 3600 rpm.

Transmission: Single-disc diaphragm clutch and four-speed manual gearbox. Front-wheel drive.

Suspension: Front, independent with MacPherson struts, trailing arms, coil springs and telescopic shock absorbers. Rear, independent with trailing arms, coil springs and telescopic shock absorbers.

Steering: Rack and pinion.

Brakes: Discs front, drums rear, servo-assisted.

Tyres: 155 SR-13.

Dimensions: Length 3889 mm (153.1 in), width 1620 mm (63.8 in), height 1359 mm (53.5 in), wheelbase 2395 mm (94.3 in).

Unladen weight: 775 kg (1708 lb).

Notes: Standard equipment includes fabric upholstery, tinted glass, radio, quartz clock, locking fuel filler cap, halogen headlamps and plastic wheelarch protectors.

DATSUN (J)   Sunny 1.5 GL 4-door

Identification: Larger-engined replacement for 1.4 GL saloon, augmenting 1.2 GL version and also available with two-door saloon, three-door coupe and five-door estate bodywork.

Engine: Front-mounted four-cylinder in-line with pushrod-operated overhead valves and Hitachi carburettor. Bore × stroke 76 × 82 mm, displacement 1488 cc. Output 52 kW (70 bhp) @ 5200 rpm, torque 115 Nm (83 lb ft) @ 3200 rpm.

Transmission: Single-disc diaphragm clutch and four-speed manual gearbox, three-speed automatic transmission optional extra. Rear-wheel drive.

Suspension: Front, independent with MacPherson struts, coil springs, telescopic shock absorbers and anti-roll bar. Rear, live axle with trailing arms, coil springs and telescopic shock absorbers.

Steering: Recirculating ball.

Brakes: Discs front, drums rear, servo-assisted.

Tyres: 155 SR-13.

Dimensions: Length 4000 mm (157.5 in), width 1590 mm (62.6 in), height 1360 mm (53.5 in), wheelbase 2340 mm (92.1 in).

Unladen weight: 830 kg (1830 lb).

Notes: Standard equipment includes radio, tinted glass, fabric upholstery, reclining seats, front head restraints, toolkit and centre console.

DATSUN (J)   Stanza 4-door

Identification: Four-door saloon model in new range of front-wheel-drive saloons replacing Violet range, supplementing similarly powered three and five-door hatchback versions.

Engine: Front and transverse-mounted four-cylinder in-line with belt-driven overhead camshaft and Nikki carburettor. Bore × stroke 78 × 83.6 mm, displacement 1585 cc. Output 60 kW (81 bhp) @ 5200 rpm, torque 130 Nm (94 lb ft) @ 3200 rpm.

Transmission: Single-disc diaphragm clutch and four-speed manual gearbox. Front-wheel drive.

Suspension: Front, independent with MacPherson struts, coil springs, telescopic shock absorbers and anti-roll bar. Rear, independent with parallel links, tie bars, coil springs and telescopic shock absorbers.

Steering: Rack and pinion.

Brakes: Ventilated discs front, drums rear, servo-assisted.

Tyres: 185/70 SR–13.

Dimensions: Length 4280 mm (168.5 in), width 1665 mm (65.6 in), height 1360 mm (53.2 in), wheelbase 2470 mm (97.2 in).

Unladen weight: 930 kg (2050 lb).

Notes: Standard equipment includes fabric upholstery, head restraints, digital quartz clock, reversible map-reading lamp, full instrumentation and remote-control luggage compartment and fuel-filler release.

DATSUN (J)

Stanza 5-door

Identification: Five-door hatchback model in new Stanza range, augmenting three-door hatchback and four-door conventional saloon versions and replacing former Violet series.

Engine: Front and transverse-mounted four-cylinder in-line with belt-driven overhead camshaft and Nikki carburettor. Bore × stroke 78 × 83.6 mm, displacement 1585 cc. Output 60 kW (81 bhp) @ 5200 rpm, torque 130 Nm (94 lb ft) @ 3200 rpm.

Transmission: Single-disc diaphragm clutch and five-speed manual gearbox. Front-wheel drive.

Suspension: Front, independent with MacPherson struts, coil springs, telescopic shock absorbers and anti-roll bar. Rear, independent with parallel links, tie bars, coil springs and telescopic shock absorbers.

Steering: Rack and pinion.

Brakes: Ventilated discs front, drums rear, servo-assisted.

Tyres: 185/70 SR–13.

Dimensions: Length 4280 mm (168.5 in), width 1665 mm (65.6 in), height 1350 mm (53.2 in), wheelbase 2470 mm (97.2 in).

Unladen weight: 950 kg (2094 lb).

Notes: Standard equipment includes fabric upholstery, head restraints, removable rear seat backs, luggage compartment cover, rear screen wash/wipe and full instrumentation.

DATSUN (J)　　　Bluebird 1.8 GL Saloon

Identification: Larger-engined of two Bluebird four-door saloons, supplementing 1.6-litre version, and augmenting similarly powered five-door estate and twin-carburettor two-door coupe.

Engine: Front-mounted four-cylinder in-line with chain-driven overhead camshaft and Nikki carburettor. Bore × stroke 85 × 78 mm, displacement 1770 cc. Output 65 kW (88 bhp) @ 5600 rpm, torque 138 Nm (98 lb ft) @ 3600 rpm.

Transmission: Single-disc diaphragm clutch and four-speed manual gearbox, three-speed automatic transmission optional extra. Rear-wheel drive.

Suspension: Front, independent with MacPherson struts, coil springs, telescopic shock absorbers and anti-roll bar. Rear independent with trailing arms, coil springs, telescopic shock absorbers and anti-roll bar.

Steering: Rack and pinion.

Brakes: Ventilated discs front, drums rear, servo-assisted.

Tyres: 165 SR–14.

Dimensions: Length 4350 mm (171.3 in), width 1656 mm (65.2 in), height 1400 mm (55.1 in), wheelbase 2525 mm (99.4 in).

Unladen weight: 1055 kg (2325 lb).

Notes: Standard equipment includes fabric upholstery, carpeted luggage compartment, centre console, driver's seat height adjustment and digital date clock.

DATSUN (J)

Identification: Smaller-engined addition to range of rebodied four-door saloons, supplementing 2.4-litre model and distinguishable by use of steel rather than alloy wheels.

Engine: Front-mounted six-cylinder in-line with chain-driven overhead camshaft and Hitachi carburettor. Bore × stroke 78 × 69.7 mm, displacement 1998 cc. Output 72 kW (96 bhp) @ 5200 rpm, torque 138 Nm (100 lb ft) @ 3600 rpm.

Transmission: Single-disc diaphragm clutch and five-speed manual gearbox, three-speed automatic transmission optional extra. Rear-wheel drive.

Suspension: Front, independent with MacPherson struts, coil springs, telescopic shock absorbers and anti-roll bar. Rear, live axle with four links, coil springs and telescopic shock absorbers.

Steering: Recirculating ball, power-assisted.

Brakes: Ventilated discs front, drums rear, servo-assisted.

Tyres: 185/70 SR–14.

Dimensions: Length 4636 mm (182.5 in), width 1689 mm (66.5 in), height 1400 mm (55.1 in), wheelbase 2670 mm (105.1 in).

Unladen weight: 1130 kg (2491 lb).

Notes: Standard equipment includes radio/stereo cassette player, tinted glass, headlamp wash/wipe, halogen headlamps and interior release for luggage compartment and fuel filler cover.

DATSUN (J)

Laurel 2.4

Identification: Top model in restyled range of four-door saloons with 2.4-litre engine supplementing alternative 2-litre version and with high level of interior equipment.

Engine: Front-mounted six-cylinder in-line with chain-driven overhead camshaft and Hitachi carburettor. Bore × stroke 83 × 73.7 mm, displacement 2393 cc. Output 85 kW (113 bhp) @ 5200 rpm, torque 177 Nm (128 lb ft) @ 3200 rpm.

Transmission: Single-disc diaphragm clutch and five-speed manual gearbox, three-speed automatic transmission optional extra. Rear-wheel drive.

Suspension: Front, independent with MacPherson struts, coil springs, telescopic shock absorbers and anti-roll bar. Rear, live axle with four links, coil springs and telescopic shock absorbers.

Steering: Recirculating ball, power-assisted.

Brakes: Ventilated discs front, drums rear, servo-assisted.

Tyres: 185/70 SR–14.

Dimensions: Length 4636 mm (182.5 in), width 1689 mm (66.5 in), height 1400 mm (55.1 in), wheelbase 2670 mm (105.1 in).

Unladen weight: 1160 kg (2557 lb).

Notes: Standard equipment includes radio, cassette player, electric window lifts and door mirror adjustment, central locking, interior fuel-filler and luggage compartment release and quartz clock.

DATSUN (J)

280 C Saloon

Identification: Flagship of Datsun saloon range incorporating 2.8-litre engine used in higher-performance form in ZX coupe series and also available as five-door estate car.

Engine: Front-mounted six-cylinder in-line with chain-driven overhead camshaft and Hitachi carburettor. Bore × stroke 86 × 79 mm, displacement 2753 cc. Output 92 kW (125 bhp) @ 4800 rpm, torque 203 Nm (145 lb ft) @ 3200 rpm.

Transmission: Three-speed automatic transmission or single-disc diaphragm clutch and five-speed manual gearbox to special order with cost reduction. Rear-wheel drive.

Suspension: Front, independent with wishbones, coil springs, telescopic shock absorbers and anti-roll bar. Rear, live axle with trailing arms, coil springs, telescopic shock absorbers and anti-roll bar.

Steering: Recirculating ball, power-assisted.

Brakes: Discs front and rear, servo-assisted.

Tyres: 195/70 HR–14.

Dimensions: Length 4815 mm (189.6 in), width 1715 mm (67.5 in), height 1430 mm (56.3 in), wheelbase 2690 mm (105.9 in).

Unladen weight: 1375 kg (3031 lb).

Notes: Standard equipment includes air-conditioning, alloy wheels, electric window lifts, central locking and radio/stereo cassette player.

DATSUN (J)

280 ZX Targa

Identification: Latest version of two-plus-two coupé incorporating twin removable centre roof panels, supplementing conventional hardtop coupés in two-seater and two-plus-two forms.

Engine: Front-mounted six-cylinder in-line with chain-driven overhead camshaft and Bosch electronic fuel injection. Bore × stroke 86 × 79 mm, displacement 2753 cc. Output 105 kW (140 bhp) @ 5200 rpm, torque 206 Nm (149 lb ft) @ 4000 rpm.

Transmission: Single-disc diaphragm clutch and five-speed manual gearbox, three-speed automatic transmission optional extra. Rear-wheel drive.

Suspension: Front, independent with MacPherson struts, coil springs, telescopic shock absorbers and anti-roll bar. Rear independent with trailing arms, coil springs, telescopic shock absorbers and anti-roll bar.

Steering: Recirculating ball, power-assisted.

Brakes: Ventilated discs front, discs rear, servo-assisted.

Tyres: 195/70 VR–14.

Dimensions: Length 4539 mm (178.7 in), width 1689 mm (66.5 in), height 1300 mm (51.2 in), wheelbase 2520 mm (99.2 in).

Unladen weight: 1240 kg (2734 lb).

Notes: Standard equipment includes fabric upholstery, reclining seats, electric window lifts, headlamp washers, radio with electric aerial, halogen headlamps and interior tailgate release.

FERRARI (I)   308 GTBi

Identification: Improved version of 308 GTB incorporating fuel-injected engine and interior changes including redesigned seats, lighter-acting clutch and more accessible gear-lever.

Engine: Centrally and transverse-mounted V-8-cylinder with four belt-driven overhead camshafts and Bosch K-Jetronic fuel injection. Bore × stroke 81 × 71 mm, displacement 2927 cc. Output 158 kW (214 bhp) @ 6600 rpm, torque 243 Nm (179 lb ft) @ 4600 rpm.

Transmission: Single-disc diaphragm clutch and five-speed manual gearbox. Rear-wheel drive.

Suspension: Front, independent with wishbones, coil springs, telescopic shock absorbers and anti-roll bar. Rear, independent with wishbones, coil springs, telescopic shock absorbers and anti-roll bar.

Steering: Rack and pinion.

Brakes: Ventilated discs front and rear, servo-assisted.

Tyres: 240/55 VR–390.

Dimensions: Length 4230 mm (166.5 in), width 1720 mm (67.7 in), height 1120 mm (44.1 in), wheelbase 2340 mm (92.1 in).

Unladen weight: 1286 kg (2835 lb).

Notes: Standard equipment includes alloy wheels, leather upholstery, electronic rev counter and speedometer, quartz clock and electrically operated window lifts, door locks and rear-view mirror.

FERRARI (I)

Identification: Open-topped alternative to 308 GTBi incorporating similar fuel-injected engine and changes to transmission controls and interior equipment.

Engine: Centrally and transverse-mounted V-8-cylinder with four belt-driven overhead camshafts and Bosch K-Jetronic fuel injection. Bore × stroke 81 × 71 mm, displacement 2927 cc. Output 158 kW (214 bhp) @ 6600 rpm, torque 243 Nm (179 lb ft) @ 4600 rpm.

Transmission: Single-disc diaphragm clutch and five-speed manual gearbox. Rear-wheel drive.

Suspension: Front, independent with wishbones, coil springs, telescopic shock absorbers and anti-roll bar. Rear, independent with wishbones, coil springs, telescopic shock absorbers and anti-roll bar.

Steering: Rack and pinion.

Brakes: Ventilated discs front and rear, servo-assisted.

Tyres: 240/55 VR–390.

Dimensions: Length 4230 mm (166.5 in), width 1720 mm (67.7 in), height 1120 mm (44.1 in), wheelbase 2340 mm (92.1 in).

Unladen weight: 1297 kg (2859 lb).

Notes: Standard equipment includes alloy wheels, leather upholstery, electronic rev counter and speedometer, quartz clock and electrically operated window lifts, door locks and rear-view mirror.

FIAT (I)   Panda 45

Identification: Economical and versatile three-door hatchback, bridging gap between 126 and 127 ranges and also available in certain markets with 652-cc twin-cylinder air-cooled engine.

Engine: Front and transverse-mounted four-cylinder in-line with pushrod-operated overhead valves and Solex or Weber carburettor. Bore × stroke 65 × 68 mm, displacement 903 cc. Output 33 kW (45 bhp) @ 5600 rpm, torque 64 Nm (47 lb ft) @ 3000 rpm.

Transmission: Single-disc diaphragm clutch and four-speed manual gearbox. Front-wheel drive.

Suspension: Front, independent with MacPherson struts, coil springs, telescopic shock absorbers and anti-roll bar. Rear, dead axle with semi-elliptic springs and telescopic shock absorbers.

Steering: Rack and pinion.

Brakes: Discs front, drums rear.

Tyres: 135 SR–13.

Dimensions: Length 3380 mm (133.1 in), width 1460 mm (57.5 in), height 1440 mm (56.7 in), wheelbase 2160 mm (85 in).

Unladen weight: 680 kg (1499 lb).

Notes: Standard equipment includes folding and removable rear seat, front, rear and side body protective mouldings, reclining front seats, tinted glass, rear screen washer and fabric upholstery.

FIAT (I)

Identification: Addition to 127 range, replacing 1050 CL and incorporating features from limited-edition Palio model and 127 Sport.

Engine: Front and transverse-mounted four-cylinder in-line with belt-driven overhead camshaft and Solex or Weber carburettor. Bore × stroke 76 × 57.8 mm, displacement 1049 cc. Output 37 kW (50 bhp) @ 5600 rpm, torque 77 Nm (57 lb ft) @ 3000 rpm.

Transmission: Single-disc diaphragm clutch and four-speed manual gearbox. Front-wheel drive.

Suspension: Front, independent with MacPherson struts, coil springs, telescopic shock absorbers and anti-roll bar. Rear, independent with MacPherson struts, transverse leaf spring and telescopic shock absorbers.

Steering: Rack and pinion.

Brakes: Discs front, drums rear, servo-assisted.

Tyres: 135 SR–13.

Dimensions: Length 3645 mm (143.5 in), width 1530 mm (60.2 in), height 1354 mm (53.3 in), wheelbase 2225 mm (87.6 in).

Unladen weight: 730 kg (1609 lb).

Notes: Standard equipment includes reclining front seats, tweed upholstery, radio, full carpeting, head restraints, door mirrors, hinged rear side windows and rear screen wash/wipe.

FIAT (BR)   127 Panorama Diesel

Identification: Diesel-engined derivative of 127 petrol-engined range, available in selected markets in choice of three-door estate and three-door hatchback forms and manufactured in Brazil.

Engine: Front and transverse-mounted four-cylinder in-line with belt-driven overhead camshaft and Bosch diesel injection. Bore × stroke 76.1 × 71.5 mm, displacement 1301 cc. Output 33 kW (44 bhp) @ 5000 rpm, torque 75 Nm (54 lb ft) @ 3000 rpm.

Transmission: Single-disc diaphragm clutch and four-speed manual gearbox. Front-wheel drive.

Suspension: Front, independent with MacPherson struts, coil springs, telescopic shock absorbers and anti-roll bar. Rear, independent with MacPherson struts, transverse leaf spring and telescopic shock absorbers.

Steering: Rack and pinion.

Brakes: Discs front, drums rear.

Tyres: 145 SR–13.

Dimensions: Length 3920 mm (154.3 in), width 1545 mm (60.8 in), height 1425 mm (56.1 in), wheelbase 2225 mm (87.6 in).

Unladen weight: 870 kg (1917 lb).

Notes: Standard equipment includes reclining front and folding rear seats, carpeted luggage compartment and roll curtain for luggage area.

FIAT (I)

Strada Super 85

Identification: Up-market addition to range of Ritmo/Strada five-door saloons, supplementing L and CL versions with higher level of performance and equipment, also available as Super 75 with 1.3-litre engine.

Engine: Front and transverse-mounted four-cylinder in-line with belt-driven overhead camshaft and Weber twin-choke carburettor. Bore × stroke 86.4 × 63.9 mm, displacement 1498 cc. Output 63 kW (85 bhp) @ 5800 rpm, torque 118 Nm (85 lb ft) @ 3800 rpm.

Transmission: Single-disc diaphragm clutch and five-speed manual gearbox, three-speed automatic transmission optional extra. Front-wheel drive.

Suspension: Front, independent with MacPherson struts, coil springs, telescopic shock absorbers and anti-roll bar. Rear, independent with MacPherson struts, transverse leaf spring, telescopic shock absorbers and anti-roll bar.

Steering: Rack and pinion.

Brakes: Discs front, drums rear, servo-assisted.

Tyres: 165/65 SR–14, 165/70 SR–13 optional extra.

Dimensions: Length 3937 mm (155 in), width 1650 mm (65 in), height 1400 mm (55.1 in), wheelbase 2448 mm (96.4 in).

Unladen weight: 930 kg (2050 lb).

Notes: Standard equipment includes height-adjustable halogen headlamps, rear screen wash/wipe, adjustable front head restraints, height-adjustable steering wheel, digital clock and carpeted luggage compartment.

FIAT (I)   Strada 105 TC

Identification: High-performance addition to Ritmo/Strada range based on three-door saloon bodywork with styling changes and powered by 1.6-litre twin-cam engine.

Engine: Front and transverse-mounted four-cylinder in-line with twin belt-driven overhead camshafts and Weber twin-choke carburettor. Bore × stroke 84 × 71.5 mm, displacement 1585 cc. Output 72 kW (105 bhp) @ 6100 rpm, torque 133 Nm (96 lb ft) @ 4000 rpm.

Transmission: Single-disc diaphragm clutch and five-speed manual gearbox. Front-wheel drive.

Suspension: Front, independent with MacPherson struts, coil springs, telescopic shock absorbers and anti-roll bar. Rear, independent with MacPherson struts, transverse leaf spring, telescopic shock absorbers and anti-roll bar.

Steering: Rack and pinion.

Brakes: Discs front, drums rear, servo-assisted.

Tyres: 165/65 SR–14, 185/60 HR–14 optional extra.

Dimensions: Length 3937 mm (155 in), width 1688 mm (66.5 in), height 1390 mm (54.7 in), wheelbase 2448 mm (96.4 in).

Unladen weight: 950 kg (2094 lb).

Notes: Standard equipment includes dual headlamps, front spoiler, centre console, rev counter, digital clock, sports steering wheel, adjustable front head restraints, rear screen wash/wipe and height-adjustable steering wheel.

FIAT (I)   Ritmo Abarth

Identification: High-performance addition to Ritmo/Strada range combining three-door bodywork with 2-litre twin-overhead-camshaft engine and uprated chassis specification.

Engine: Front and transverse-mounted four-cylinder in-line with twin belt-driven overhead camshafts and Weber twin-choke carburettor. Bore × stroke 84 × 90 mm, displacement 1995 cc. Output 92 kW (125 bhp) @ 5800 rpm, torque 172 Nm (124 lb ft) @ 3500 rpm.

Transmission: Single-disc diaphragm clutch and five-speed manual gearbox. Front-wheel drive.

Suspension: Front, independent with MacPherson struts, coil springs, telescopic shock absorbers and anti-roll bar. Rear, independent with MacPherson struts, transverse leaf spring, telescopic shock absorbers and anti-roll bar.

Steering: Rack and pinion.

Brakes: Ventilated discs front, drums rear, servo-assisted.

Tyres: 185/60 HR–14.

Dimensions: Length 3937 mm (155 in), width 1688 mm (66.5 in), height 1380 mm (54.3 in), wheelbase 2448 mm (96.4 in).

Unladen weight: 980 kg (2160 lb).

Notes: Standard equipment includes fabric upholstery, head restraints, alloy wheels, full instrumentation, adjustable-height three-spoke steering wheel and rear screen wash/wipe.

FIAT (I)   131 Mirafiori 1400 CL

Identification: Smallest-engined model in revised and restructured 131 range of four-door saloons and five-door estates, replacing 1300 models and also available with 1.6-litre version of new engine.

Engine: Front-mounted four-cylinder in-line with belt-driven overhead camshaft and Solex or Weber twin-choke carburettor. Bore × stroke 78 × 71.5 mm, displacement 1367 cc. Output 52 kW (70 bhp) @ 5500 rpm, torque 108 Nm (78 lb ft) @ 3000 rpm.

Transmission: Single-disc diaphragm clutch and four-speed manual gearbox, five-speed manual gearbox optional extra. Rear-wheel drive.

Suspension: Front, independent with MacPherson struts, coil springs, telescopic shock absorbers and anti-roll bar. Rear, live axle with trailing arms, Panhard rod, coil springs and telescopic shock absorbers.

Steering: Rack and pinion.

Brakes: Discs front, drums rear, servo-assisted.

Tyres: 165 SR–13.

Dimensions: Length 4264 mm (167.9 in), width 1644 mm (64.7 in), height 1411 mm (55.6 in), wheelbase 2490 mm (98 in).

Unladen weight: 1025 kg (2259 lb).

Notes: Standard equipment includes internally adjustable door mirror, head restraints, body side protection strips and bumper corner pads, fabric upholstery and illuminated glove compartment.

FIAT (I)   131 Supermirafiori 2000 TC

Identification: High-performance model in twin-cam-engined Supermirafiori range, supplementing 1400 and 1600 versions and also available as Panorama five-door estate.

Engine: Front-mounted four-cylinder in-line with twin belt-driven overhead camshafts and Weber twin-choke carburettor. Bore × stroke 84 × 90 mm, displacement 1995 cc. Output 83 kW (113 bhp) @ 5600 rpm, torque 167 Nm (121 lb ft) @ 3600 rpm.

Transmission: Single-disc diaphragm clutch and five-speed manual gearbox. Rear-wheel drive.

Suspension: Front, independent with MacPherson struts, coil springs, telescopic shock absorbers and anti-roll bar. Rear, live axle with trailing arms, Panhard rod, coil springs and telescopic shock absorbers.

Steering: Rack and pinion.

Brakes: Discs front, drums rear, servo-assisted.

Tyres: 185/70 SR–13 or 185/65 SR–13.

Dimensions: Length 4230 mm (166.5 in), width 1646 mm (64.8 in), height 1405 mm (55.3 in), wheelbase 2490 mm (98 in).

Unladen weight: 1080 kg (2380 lb).

Notes: Standard equipment includes front and rear head restraints, electric window lifts and door locks, centre console, remote-control gear-lever and body side protection panels.

FIAT (I) 131 Panorama Super Diesel

Identification: Largest-engined model in revised Supermirafiori range, also available as four-door saloon and combining high level of equipment with 2½-litre diesel engine.

Engine: Front-mounted four-cylinder in-line with belt-driven overhead camshaft and Bosch diesel injection. Bore × stroke 93 × 90 mm, displacement 2445 cc. Output 53 kW (72 bhp) @ 4200 rpm, torque 147 Nm (106 lb ft) @ 2400 rpm.

Transmission: Single-disc diaphragm clutch and five-speed manual gearbox. Rear-wheel drive.

Suspension: Front, independent with MacPherson struts, coil springs, telescopic shock absorbers and anti-roll bar. Rear, live axle with trailing arms, Panhard rod, coil springs and telescopic shock absorbers.

Steering: Rack and pinion, power-assisted.

Brakes: Discs front, drums rear, servo-assisted.

Tyres: 165 SR–13.

Dimensions: Length 4230 mm (166.5 in), width 1646 mm (64.8 in), height 1420 mm (55.9 in), wheelbase 2490 mm (98 in).

Unladen weight: 1220 kg (2689 lb).

Notes: Standard equipment includes rear screen wash/wipe, body side protection panels, internally adjustable door mirror, electric window lifts and door locks and dual headlamps.

FIAT (I)   Argenta 2000

Identification: New flagship of Fiat range, also offered in 1600, 2000i (fuel-injected) and 2500D (diesel) forms, based on former 132 design, but with significantly higher specification and many styling changes.

Engine: Front-mounted four-cylinder in-line with twin belt-driven overhead camshafts and Weber twin-choke carburettor. Bore × stroke 84 × 90 mm, displacement 1995 cc. Output 83 kW (111 bhp) @ 5600 rpm, torque 167 Nm (121 lb ft) @ 3700 rpm.

Transmission: Single-disc diaphragm clutch and five-speed manual gearbox, three-speed automatic transmission optional extra. Rear-wheel drive.

Suspension: Front, independent with wishbones, coil springs, telescopic shock absorbers and anti-roll bar. Rear, live axle with trailing arms, Panhard rod, coil springs and telescopic shock absorbers.

Steering: Recirculating ball, power-assisted.

Brakes: Discs front, drums rear, servo-assisted.

Tyres: 175/70 SR–14 or 175/70 HR–14.

Dimensions: Length 4449 mm (175.2 in), width 1650 mm (65 in), height 1420 mm (55.9 in), wheelbase 2558 mm (100.7 in).

Unladen weight: 1180 kg (2601 lb).

Notes: Standard equipment includes electric front window lifts and central door locking, econometer, function check panel, digital clock, front and rear head restraints and carpeted luggage compartment.

FORD (GB & E)   Fiesta Popular

Identification: Additional model at lower end of Fiesta range, also available with higher-compression engine or as Popular Plus with similar engine or 1.1-litre version and higher level of equipment.

Engine: Front and transverse-mounted four-cylinder in-line with pushrod-operated overhead valves and Ford carburettor. Bore × stroke 74 × 55.7 mm, displacement 957 cc. Output 30 kW (40 bhp) @ 5500 rpm, torque 65 Nm (47 lb ft) @ 2700 rpm.

Transmission: Single-disc diaphragm clutch and four-speed manual gearbox. Front-wheel drive.

Suspension: Front, independent with MacPherson struts, coil springs and telescopic shock absorbers. Rear, dead axle with trailing arms, coil springs and telescopic shock absorbers.

Steering: Rack and pinion.

Brakes: Discs front, drums rear.

Tyres: 135 SR–12.

Dimensions: Length 3566 mm (140.4 in), width 1567 mm (61.7 in), height 1313 mm (51.7 in), wheelbase 2286 mm (90 in).

Unladen weight: 700 kg (1542 lb).

Notes: Standard equipment includes black door locks and handles, vinyl upholstery, rubber floor mats, black wheel-nut caps and side tape stripe.

FORD (GB & E)　　　Fiesta Popular Plus 1.1

Identification: Larger-engined of two Popular Plus models, supplementing 957-cc version and based on Popular, but with higher level of trim and equipment.

Engine: Front and transverse-mounted four-cylinder in-line with pushrod-operated overhead valves and Ford carburettor. Bore × stroke 74 × 65 mm, displacement 1117 cc. Output 40 kW (53 bhp) @ 6000 rpm, torque 82 Nm (59 lb ft) @ 3000 rpm.

Transmission: Single-disc diaphragm clutch and four-speed manual gearbox. Front-wheel drive.

Suspension: Front, independent with MacPherson struts, coil springs and telescopic shock absorbers. Rear, dead axle with trailing arms, coil springs and telescopic shock absorbers.

Steering: Rack and pinion.

Brakes: Discs front, drums rear, servo-assisted.

Tyres: 145 SR–12.

Dimensions: Length 3566 mm (140.4 in), width 1567 mm (61.7 in), height 1313 mm (51.7 in), wheelbase 2286 mm (90 in).

Unladen weight: 722 kg (1591 lb).

Notes: Standard equipment includes tailgate wash/wipe, centre console and clock, fabric upholstery, rear package tray, carpets, courtesy light, rear wheelarch covers and passenger sun visor.

FORD (GB & E)   Fiesta 1.3 S

Identification: Larger-engined of two S versions in improved Fiesta range, supplementing 1.1-litre model and distinguishable by new sports road wheels and revised bumpers.

Engine: Front and transverse-mounted four-cylinder in-line with pushrod-operated overhead valves and Ford carburettor. Bore × stroke 81 × 63 mm, displacement 1298 cc. Output 49 kW (66 bhp) @ 5600 rpm, torque 94 Nm (68 lb ft) @ 3250 rpm.

Transmission: Single-disc diaphragm clutch and four-speed manual gearbox. Front-wheel drive.

Suspension: Front, independent with MacPherson struts, coil springs and telescopic shock absorbers. Rear, dead axle with trailing arms, coil springs, telescopic shock absorbers and anti-roll bar.

Steering: Rack and pinion.

Brakes: Discs front, drums rear, servo-assisted.

Tyres: 155/70 SR–13.

Dimensions: Length 3566 mm (140.4 in), width 1567 mm (61.7 in), height 1313 mm (51.7 in), wheelbase 2286 mm (90 in).

Unladen weight: 775 kg (1708 lb).

Notes: Standard equipment includes rear screen wash/wipe, front head restraints, fabric upholstery, centre console, radio, halogen headlamps and rev counter.

FORD (GB & E)   Fiesta XR2

Identification: High-performance addition to Fiesta range, replacing Supersport model and combining 1.6-litre engine with aerodynamic body changes and uprated suspension and brakes.

Engine: Front and transverse-mounted four-cylinder in-line with pushrod-opererated overhead valves and Weber twin-choke carburettor. Bore × stroke 87.7 × 66 mm, displacement 1593 cc. Output 63 kW (84 bhp) @ 5500 rpm, torque 124 Nm (90 lb ft) @ 2800 rpm.

Transmission: Single-disc diaphragm clutch and four-speed manual gearbox. Front-wheel drive.

Suspension: Front, independent with MacPherson struts, coil springs and telescopic shock absorbers. Rear, dead axle with trailing arms, coil springs, telescopic shock absorbers and anti-roll bar.

Steering: Rack and pinion.

Brakes: Ventilated discs front, drums rear, servo-assisted.

Tyres: 185/60 HR–12.

Dimensions: Length 3566 mm (140.4 in), width 1567 mm (61.7 in), height 1313 mm (51.7 in), wheelbase 2286 mm (90 in).

Unladen weight: 785 kg (1730 lb).

Notes: Standard equipment includes electronic ignition, extended wheelarches, front and rear spoilers, circular headlamps, fabric upholstery, reclining front seats and carpeted floor and rear package tray.

FORD (D)   Escort XR3

Identification: High-performance model of Escort range combining modified three-door bodyshell with 1.6-litre engine and uprated running gear.

Engine: Front and transverse-mounted four-cylinder in-line with belt-driven overhead camshaft and Weber twin-choke carburettor. Bore × stroke 80 × 79.5 mm, displacement 1596 cc. Output 71 kW (96 bhp) @ 6000 rpm, torque 133 Nm (98 lb ft) @ 4000 rpm.

Transmission: Single-disc diaphragm clutch and four-speed manual gearbox. Front-wheel drive.

Suspension: Front, independent with MacPherson struts, coil springs, gas-filled telescopic shock absorbers and anti-roll bar. Rear, independent with coil springs, transverse arms, longitudinal tie bars and gas-filled telescopic shock absorbers.

Steering: Rack and pinion.

Brakes: Ventilated discs front, drums rear, servo-assisted.

Tyres: 185/60 HR–14.

Dimensions: Length 3970 mm (156.3 in), width 1588 mm (62.5 in), height 1336 mm (52.6 in), wheelbase 2398 mm (94.4 in).

Unladen weight: 895 kg (1973 lb).

Notes: Standard equipment includes front and rear spoilers, wheelarch deflectors, Recaro reclining seats, fabric upholstery, head restraints, luggage compartment cover and alloy wheels.

FORD (GB)   Cortina 1300 L

Identification: Intermediate model between base and GL Cortinas, also available with 1.6-litre engine and with choice of two-door saloon and five-door estate bodywork, all with uprated specification.

Engine: Front-mounted four-cylinder in-line with pushrod-operated overhead valves and Ford carburettor. Bore × stroke 81 × 63 mm, displacement 1297 cc. Output 45 kW (60 bhp) @ 5750 rpm, torque 94 Nm (68 lb ft) @ 3000 rpm.

Transmission: Single-disc diaphragm clutch and four-speed manual gearbox. Rear-wheel drive.

Suspension: Front, independent with wishbones, coil springs, telescopic shock absorbers and anti-roll bar. Rear, live axle with trailing arms, coil springs, telescopic shock absorbers and anti-roll bar.

Steering: Rack and pinion.

Brakes: Discs front, drums rear, servo-assisted.

Tyres: 165 SR–13.

Dimensions: Length 4340 mm (170.0 in), width 1700 mm (66.9 in), height 1360 mm (53.5 in), wheelbase 2578 mm (101.5 in).

Unladen weight: 1000 kg (2204 lb).

Notes: Standard equipment includes radio, fabric upholstery, head restraints, halogen headlamps, clock, rear centre armrest, passenger door mirror and centre console.

FORD (D)   *Capri 1600 LS*

Identification: New model, replacing 1.6-litre Capri S and supplementing similarly powered L and GL versions and 2-litre GL and S models.

Engine: Front-mounted four-cylinder in-line with belt-driven overhead camshaft and Ford carburettor. Bore × stroke 87.6 × 66 mm, displacement 1593 cc. Output 55 kW (73 bhp) @ 5300 rpm, torque 120 Nm (87 lb ft) @ 2700 rpm.

Transmission: Single-disc diaphragm clutch and four-speed manual gearbox. Rear-wheel drive.

Suspension: Front, independent with MacPherson struts, coil springs, telescopic shock absorbers and anti-roll bar. Rear, live axle with semi-elliptic springs and telescopic shock absorbers.

Steering: Rack and pinion.

Brakes: Discs front, drums rear, servo-assisted.

Tyres: 185/70 SR–13.

Dimensions: Length 4374 mm (172.2 in), width 1700 mm (66.9 in), height 1288 mm (50.7 in), wheelbase 2563 mm (100.9 in).

Unladen weight: 1000 kg (2204 lb).

Notes: Standard equipment includes tailgate spoiler, sports road wheels, S suspension pack, rear package tray and fabric upholstery.

FORD (D)   *Capri 2.8 Injection*

Identification: New top model in Capri range, based on S model, but with 2.8-litre fuel-injected V-6 engine and extensively developed suspension.

Engine: Front-mounted V-6-cylinder with pushrod-operated overhead valves and Bosch K–Jetronic fuel injection. Bore × stroke 93 × 68.5 mm, displacement 2792 cc. Output 120 kW (160 bhp) @ 5700 rpm, torque 224 Nm (162 lb ft) @ 4300 rpm.

Transmission: Single-disc diaphragm clutch and four-speed manual gearbox. Rear-wheel drive.

Suspension: Front, independent with MacPherson struts, coil springs, telescopic shock absorbers and anti-roll bar. Rear, live axle with semi-elliptic springs, telescopic shock absorbers and anti-roll bar.

Steering: Rack and pinion, power-assisted.

Brakes: Ventilated discs front, drums rear, servo-assisted.

Tyres: 205/60–13.

Dimensions: Length 4440 mm (174.8 in), width 1699 mm (66.9 in), height 1288 mm (50.7 in), wheelbase 2563 mm (100.9 in).

Unladen weight: 1190 kg, (2623 lb).

Notes: Standard equipment includes alloy wheels, rear spoiler, stereo radio/cassette player, sports steering wheel, Recaro contoured seats, extra sound insulation and heavy-duty brakes.

FORD (D)

Granada 2.0 L

Identification: Smallest-engined model in revised Granada range incorporating minor styling changes and improved mechanical specification including retuned suspension, steering and brakes.

Engine: Front-mounted four-cylinder in-line with belt-driven overhead camshaft and Weber carburettor. Bore × stroke 90.8 × 77 mm, displacement 1998 cc. Output 76 kW (101 bhp) @ 5200 rpm, torque 156 Nm (113 lb ft) @ 4000 rpm.

Transmission: Single-disc diaphragm clutch and four-speed manual gearbox, three-speed automatic transmission optional extra. Rear-wheel drive.

Suspension: Front, independent with wishbones, coil springs, telescopic shock absorbers and anti-roll bar. Rear, independent with trailing arms, coil springs and telescopic shock absorbers.

Steering: Rack and pinion, power assistance optional extra.

Brakes: Discs front, drums rear, servo-assisted.

Tyres: 175 SR–14.

Dimensions: Length 4653 mm (183.2 in), width 1793 mm (70.6 in), height 1379 mm (54.3 in), wheelbase 2769 mm (109 in).

Unladen weight: 1185 kg (2612 lb).

Notes: Standard equipment includes electronic ignition, halogen headlamps, radio, front head restraints, velour fabric upholstery and remote-control driver's door mirror.

FORD (D)

Granada 2.3 GL Estate

Identification: Intermediate model in revised range of Granada estates, bridging gap between L and Ghia or Injection models and also available with 2.0-litre or 2.8-litre engines.

Engine: Front-mounted V-6-cylinder with pushrod-operated overhead valves and Solex carburettor. Bore × stroke 90 × 60.1 mm, displacement 2294 cc. Output 84 kW (114 bhp) @ 5300 rpm, torque 181 Nm (129 lb ft) @ 3000 rpm.

Transmission: Single-disc diaphragm clutch and four-speed manual gearbox, three-speed automatic transmission optional extra. Rear-wheel drive.

Suspension: Front, independent with wishbones, coil springs, telescopic shock absorbers and anti-roll bar. Rear, independent with trailing arms, coil springs and telescopic shock absorbers.

Steering: Rack and pinion, power-assisted.

Brakes: Ventilated discs front, drums rear, servo-assisted.

Tyres: 185/70 SR–14.

Dimensions: Length 4760 mm (187.4 in), width 1793 mm (70.6 in), height 1370 mm (54.3 in), wheelbase 2769 mm (109 in).

Unladen weight: 1365 kg (3008 lb).

Notes: Standard equipment includes tilting/sliding sun roof, radio with front and rear speakers, central locking, velour fabric upholstery, halogen headlamps and front head restraints.

FORD (D)   Granada 2.8 Injection

Identification: Highest-performance model in revised Granada range incorporating uprated suspension and distinguishable by front and rear spoilers and special paint finish, also available in estate form.

Engine: Front-mounted V-6-cylinder with pushrod-operated overhead valves and Bosch K–Jetronic fuel injection. Bore × stroke 93 × 68.5 mm, displacement 2792 cc. Output 120 kW (160 bhp) @ 5700 rpm, torque 224 Nm (162 lb ft) × 4300 rpm.

Transmission: Single-disc diaphragm clutch and four-speed manual gearbox. Rear-wheel drive.

Suspension: Front, independent with wishbones, coil springs, telescopic shock absorbers and anti-roll bar. Rear, independent with trailing arms, coil springs, telescopic shock absorbers and anti-roll bar.

Steering: Rack and pinion, power-assisted.

Brakes: Ventilated discs front, drums rear, servo-assisted.

Tyres: 190/65 HR–390.

Dimensions: Length 4653 mm (183.2 in), width 1793 mm (70.6 in), height 1379 mm (54.3 in), wheelbase 2769 mm (109 in).

Unladen weight: 1375 kg (3030 lb).

Notes: Standard equipment includes alloy wheels, auxiliary lamps, Recaro seats, radio/stereo cassette player and overhead console.

FORD (D)

Granada 2.8 Ghia

Identification: Top-specification model in Granada saloon range, also available with 2.3-litre or 2.8-litre fuel-injected engine and distinguishable by bright front grille surround.

Engine: Front-mounted V–6-cylinder with pushrod-operated overhead valves and Weber carburettor. Bore × stroke 93 × 68.5 mm, displacement 2792 cc. Output 101 kW (135 bhp) @ 5200 rpm, torque 220 Nm (159 lb ft) @ 3000 rpm.

Transmission: Three-speed automatic transmission, four-speed manual gearbox with single-disc diaphragm clutch to special order. Rear-wheel drive.

Suspension: Front, independent with wishbones, coil springs, telescopic shock absorbers and anti-roll bar. Rear, independent with trailing arms, coil springs and telescopic shock absorbers.

Steering: Rack and pinion, power-assisted.

Brakes: Ventilated discs front, drums rear, servo-assisted.

Tyres: 190/65 HR–390.

Dimensions: Length 4653 mm (183.2 in), width 1793 mm (70.6 in), height 1379 mm (54.3 in), wheelbase 2769 mm (109 in).

Unladen weight: 1365 kg (3008 lb).

Notes: Standard equipment includes alloy wheels, electric window lifts, central locking, headlamp washers, velour upholstery and adjustable front and rear head restraints.

FRAZER (GB)   Tickford

Identification: First model of new British make, based on Mini Metro 1.3S and developed and manufactured by Aston Martin Lagonda/Tickford.

Engine: Front and transverse-mounted four-cylinder in-line with pushrod-operated overhead valves and SU carburettor. Bore × stroke 70.6 × 81.3 mm, displacement 1275 cc. Output 65 kW (87 bhp) @ 6000 rpm, torque 111 Nm (80 lb ft) @ 3000 rpm.

Transmission: Single-disc diaphragm clutch and four-speed manual gearbox. Front-wheel drive.

Suspension: Front, independent with transverse links, Hydragas units, telescopic shock absorbers and anti-roll bar. Rear, independent with trailing arms, Hydragas units with integral coil springs and shock absorbers and transverse link.

Steering: Rack and pinion.

Brakes: Discs front, drums rear, servo-assisted.

Tyres: 175/50 VR–13.

Dimensions: Length 3430 mm (135 in), width 1562 mm (61.5 in), height 1334 mm (52.5 in), wheelbase 2251 mm (88.6 in).

Unladen weight: Approx. 800 kg (1763 lb).

Notes: Standard equipment includes leather upholstery and trim, special dashboard and seats, stereo radio/cassette player, electric front window lifts, sun roof and cruise control.

GINETTA (GB) G4 Series IV

Identification: Re-introduced and revised two-seater coupe by small specialist manufacturer using glass-fibre body on tubular chassis and Ford 1.6-litre engine.

Engine: Front-mounted four-cylinder in-line with pushrod-operated overhead valves and Weber carburettor. Bore × stroke 81 × 77.6 mm, displacement 1599 cc. Output 66 kW (88 bhp) @ 5500 rpm, torque 127 Nm (92 lb ft) @ 3500 rpm.

Transmission: Single-disc diaphragm clutch and four-speed manual gearbox. Rear-wheel drive.

Suspension: Front, independent with wishbones, coil springs, telescopic shock absorbers and anti-roll bar. Rear, live axle with trailing arms, coil springs and telescopic shock absorbers.

Steering: Rack and pinion.

Brakes: Discs front, drums rear.

Tyres: 185/70 SR–13.

Dimensions: Length 3734 mm (147 in), width 1575 mm (62 in), height 1067 mm (42 in), wheelbase 2134 mm (84 in).

Unladen weight: 560 kg (1232 lb).

Notes: Standard equipment includes swivelling halogen headlamps, laminated screen, lift-up front body section, full instrumentation, alloy wheels, Vynide hood and side screens.

HONDA (J)

Civic 1300 5-door

Identification: Larger-bodied of two Civic saloons, supplementing shorter-wheelbase three-door model and available with choice of transmissions.

Engine: Front and transverse-mounted four-cylinder in-line with belt-driven overhead camshaft and Keihin carburettor. Bore × stroke 72 × 82 mm, displacement 1335 cc. Output 44 kW (60 bhp) @ 5000 rpm, torque 97 Nm (69 lb ft) @ 3500 rpm.

Transmission: Single-disc diaphragm clutch and five-speed manual gearbox, two-speed semi-automatic transmission optional extra. Front-wheel drive.

Suspension: Front, independent with MacPherson struts, coil springs, telescopic shock absorbers and anti-roll bar. Rear, independent with MacPherson struts, coil springs and telescopic shock absorbers.

Steering: Rack and pinion.

Brakes: Discs front, drums rear, servo-assisted.

Tyres: 155 SR–13.

Dimensions: Length 3830 mm (150.8 in), width 1580 mm (62.2 in), height 1335 mm (52.6 in), wheelbase 2320 mm (91.3 in).

Unladen weight: 785 kg (1730 lb).

Notes: Standard equipment includes radio, three-speed heater blower, folding rear seat, remote tailgate release and tool kit.

HONDA (J)

Identification: Three-door hatchback version of Accord range, also available with four-door saloon bodywork with two levels of equipment.

Engine: Front and transverse-mounted four-cylinder in-line with belt-driven overhead camshaft and Keihin carburettor. Bore × stroke 77 × 86 mm, displacement 1602 cc. Output 59 kW (80 bhp) @ 5300 rpm, torque 127 Nm (92 lb ft) @ 3500 rpm.

Transmission: Single-disc diaphragm clutch and five-speed manual gearbox, three-speed Hondamatic automatic transmission optional extra. Front-wheel drive.

Suspension: Front, independent with MacPherson struts, coil springs, telescopic shock absorbers and anti-roll bar. Rear, independent with MacPherson struts, coil springs, telescopic shock absorbers and anti-roll bar.

Steering: Rack and pinion.

Brakes: Discs front, drums rear, servo-assisted.

Tyres: 155 SR–13.

Dimensions: Length 4075 mm (160.4 in), width 1618 mm (63.8 in), height 1360 mm (53.5 in), wheelbase 2380 mm (93.7 in).

Unladen weight: 890 kg (1962 lb).

Notes: Standard equipment includes fabric upholstery, head restraints, digital clock, rev counter, radio, tinted glass and rear screen wash/wipe.

HONDA (J) Quintet

Identification: UK-specification version of five-door saloon based on Honda Accord three-door and four-door models with similar engine.

Engine: Front and transverse-mounted four-cylinder in-line with belt-driven overhead camshaft and Keihin twin-choke carburettor. Bore × stroke 77 × 86 mm, displacement 1602 cc. Output 59 kW (80 bhp) @ 5300 rpm, torque 130 Nm (93 lb ft) @ 3500 rpm.

Transmission: Single-disc diaphragm clutch and five-speed manual gearbox, three-speed automatic transmission optional extra. Front-wheel drive.

Suspension: Front, independent with MacPherson struts, coil springs, telescopic shock absorbers and anti-roll bar. Rear, independent with MacPherson struts, coil springs, telescopic shock absorbers and anti-roll bar.

Steering: Rack and pinion.

Brakes: Discs front, drums rear, servo-assisted.

Tyres: 155 SR–13.

Dimensions: Length 4110 mm (161.8 in), width 1615 mm (63.6 in), height 1355 mm (53.4 in), wheelbase 2360 mm (92.9 in).

Unladen weight: 895 kg (1973 lb).

Notes: Standard equipment includes electrically operated sliding roof, alloy wheels, rear screen wash/wipe, radio, door mirrors, remote tailgate release and divided rear seat backrest.

JAGUAR (GB)

Identification: Smallest-engined model in Jaguar saloon range, supplementing 4.2-litre six-cylinder and 5.3-litre V-12-engined models with similar body style.

Engine: Front-mounted six-cylinder in-line with twin chain-driven overhead camshafts and twin SU carburettors. Bore × stroke 83 × 106 mm, displacement 3442 cc. Output 120 kW (162 bhp) @ 5250 rpm, torque 261 Nm (189 lb ft) @ 4000 rpm.

Transmission: Single-disc diaphragm clutch and five-speed manual gearbox, three-speed automatic transmission optional extra. Rear-wheel drive.

Suspension: Front, independent with wishbones, coil springs, telescopic shock absorbers and anti-roll bar. Rear, independent with trailing arms, wishbones, fixed-length drive-shafts, dual coil springs and telescopic shock absorbers.

Steering: Rack and pinion, power-assisted.

Brakes: Ventilated discs front, discs rear, servo-assisted.

Tyres: 205/70 VR–15.

Dimensions: Length 4960 mm (195.2 in), width 1770 mm (69.7 in), height 1377 mm (54 in), wheelbase 2865 mm (112.8 in).

Unladen weight: 1770 kg (3900 lb).

Notes: Standard equipment includes central door locking, electric window lifts, push-button radio, fabric upholstery and adjustable front-seat lumbar support.

JAGUAR (GB)

XJ12 HE

Identification: Most powerful model in range of XJ saloons, supplementing 3.4 and 4.2 six-cylinder models and incorporating V-12 engine with Michael May-designed high-compression cylinder-heads.

Engine: Front-mounted V-12-cylinder with single chain-driven overhead camshafts and Lucas electronic digital fuel injection. Bore × stroke 90 × 70 mm, displacement 5343 cc. Output 224 kW (299 bhp) @ 5500 rpm, torque 440 Nm (318 lb ft) @ 3000 rpm.

Transmission: Three-speed automatic transmission. Rear-wheel drive.

Suspension: Front, independent with wishbones, coil springs, telescopic shock absorbers and anti-roll bar. Rear, independent with trailing arms, wishbones, fixed-length drive-shafts, dual coil springs and telescopic shock absorbers.

Steering: Rack and pinion, power-assisted.

Brakes: Ventilated discs front, discs rear, servo-assisted.

Tyres: 215/70 VR–15.

Dimensions: Length 4959 mm (195.2 in), width 1770 mm (69.7 in), height 1377 mm (54 in), wheelbase 2865 mm (112.8 in).

Unladen weight: 1930 kg (4250 lb).

Notes: Standard equipment includes alloy wheels, chrome waist mouldings and electrically controlled steel sliding roof, rear-view mirrors and headlamp wash/wipe.

JAGUAR (GB)   XJ-S HE

Identification: Improved version of V-12-engined coupe incorporating Michael May-designed high-compression cylinder-heads, revised front and rear bumpers and uprated interior specification.

Engine: Front-mounted V-12-cylinder with single chain-driven overhead camshafts and Lucas electronic digital fuel injection. Bore × stroke 90 × 70 mm, displacement 5343 cc. Output 224 kW (299 bhp) @ 5500 rpm, torque 440 Nm (318 lb ft) @ 3000 rpm.

Transmission: Three-speed automatic transmission. Rear-wheel drive.

Suspension: Front, independent with wishbones, coil springs telescopic shock absorbers and anti-roll bar. Rear, independent with trailing arms, wishbones, fixed-length drive-shafts, dual coil springs and telescopic shock absorbers.

Steering: Rack and pinion, power-assisted.

Brakes: Ventilated discs front, discs rear, servo-assisted.

Tyres: 215/70 VR-15

Dimensions: Length 4743 mm (186.8 in), width 1793 mm (70.6 in), height 1270 mm (50 in), wheelbase 2591 mm (102 in).

Unladen weight: 1770 kg (3900 lb).

Notes: Standard equipment includes alloy wheels, air-conditioning, leather upholstery and trim, electric window lifts and rear view mirror adjustment, limited-slip differential and computerized stereo radio/cassette unit.

LANCIA (I)   Delta 1500

Identification: Five-door hatchback saloon incorporating developed versions of Fiat-designed mechanical units and also available in certain markets with 1.3-litre engine.

Engine: Front and transverse-mounted four-cylinder in-line with belt-driven overhead camshaft and Weber carburettor. Bore × stroke 86.4 × 63.9 mm, displacement 1498 cc. Output 63 kW (85 bhp) @ 5800 rpm, torque 123 Nm (90 lb ft) @ 3500 rpm.

Transmission: Single-disc diaphragm clutch and five-speed manual gearbox. Front-wheel drive.

Suspension: Front, independent with MacPherson struts, coil springs, telescopic shock absorbers and anti-roll bar. Rear, independent with MacPherson struts, trailing arms, transverse links, coil springs and telescopic shock absorbers.

Steering: Rack and pinion.

Brakes: Discs front, drums rear, servo-assisted.

Tyres: 165/70 SR–13.

Dimensions: Length 3885 mm (153 in), width 1620 mm (63.8 in), height 1380 mm (54.3 in), wheelbase 2475 mm (97.4 in).

Unladen weight: 975 kg (2149 lb).

Notes: Standard equipment includes velour upholstery, split and folding rear seat, height-adjustable steering column, remote-control door mirrors and rev counter.

LANCIA (I)   Beta 2000 ES

Identification: Top model in revised range of Beta five-door saloons, supplementing 1.6-litre-engined version; Beta also available as two-door coupe or three-door HPE estate.

Engine: Front and transverse-mounted four-cylinder in-line with twin belt-driven overhead camshafts and twin-choke Weber carburettor. Bore × stroke 84 × 90 mm, displacement 1995 cc. Output 85 kW (115 bhp) @ 5500 rpm, torque 178 Nm (129 lb ft) @ 2800 rpm.

Transmission: Single-disc diaphragm clutch and five-speed manual gearbox, three-speed automatic transmission optional extra. Front-wheel drive.

Suspension: Front, independent with MacPherson struts, coil springs, telescopic shock absorbers and anti-roll bar. Rear, independent with MacPherson struts, coil springs, telescopic shock absorbers and anti-roll bar.

Steering: Rack and pinion, power-assisted.

Brakes: Discs front and rear, servo-assisted.

Tyres: 175/70 SR–14.

Dimensions: Length 4293 mm (169 in), width 1650 mm (65 in), height 1397 mm (55 in), wheelbase 2527 mm (99.5 in).

Unladen weight: 1100 kg (2424 lb).

Notes: Standard equipment includes multiple warning light system with test circuit, fabric upholstery, head restraints, tinted glass, centre console and halogen headlamps.

LANCIA (I)   Montecarlo

Identification: UK-specification version of re-introduced two-seater coupe based on Beta design and incorporating front and rear styling changes and revised window arrangements.

Engine: Centrally and transverse-mounted four-cylinder in-line with twin belt-driven overhead camshafts and twin-choke Weber carburettor. Bore × stroke 84 × 90 mm, displacement 1995 cc. Output 89 kW (120 bhp) @ 6000 rpm, torque 171 Nm (126 lb ft) @ 3400 rpm.

Transmission: Single-disc diaphragm clutch and five-speed manual gearbox. Rear-wheel drive.

Suspension: Front, independent with MacPherson struts, coil springs, telescopic shock absorbers and anti-roll bar. Rear, independent with MacPherson struts, coil springs, adjustable transverse links, telescopic shock absorbers and anti-roll bar.

Steering: Rack and pinion.

Brakes: Discs front and rear, servo-assisted.

Tyres: 185/65 HR–14.

Dimensions: Length 3815 mm (150.2 in), width 1695 mm (66.7 in), height 1190 mm (46.9 in), wheelbase 2300 mm (90.6 in).

Unladen weight: 970 kg (2138 lb).

Notes: Standard equipment includes alloy wheels, stereo radio/cassette player, electric window lifts, courtesy light delay and digital clock.

LANCIA (I)   Trevi 2000

Identification: Larger-engined of two versions of 'three-box' saloon derivative of Beta hatchback incorporating uprated mechanical and equipment specification, also available in 1.6-litre form.

Engine: Front and transverse-mounted four-cylinder in-line with twin belt-driven overhead camshafts and Weber twin-choke carburettor. Bore × stroke 84 × 90 mm, displacement 1995 cc. Output 86 kW (115 bhp) @ 5500 rpm, torque 178 Nm (129 lb ft) @ 2800 rpm.

Transmission: Single-disc diaphragm clutch and five-speed manual gearbox, three-speed automatic transmission optional extra. Front-wheel drive.

Suspension: Front, independent with MacPherson struts, coil springs, telescopic shock absorbers and anti-roll bar. Rear, independent with MacPherson struts, coil springs, telescopic shock absorbers and anti-roll bar.

Steering: Rack and pinion, power-assisted.

Brakes: Discs front and rear, servo-assisted.

Tyres: 185/65 HR-14.

Dimensions: Length 4355 mm (171.5 in), width 1706 mm (67.2 in), height 1400 mm (55.1 in), wheelbase 2540 mm (100 in).

Unladen weight: 1165 kg (2568 lb).

Notes: Standard equipment includes electric window lifts, digital quartz clock, tinted glass, alloy wheels, sliding roof, front and rear head restraints, electronic ignition and monitoring of all safety features.

LANCIA (I) Gamma 2500 Injection

Identification: Additional model to Gamma saloon range, developed from original Weber-carburettor version and supplementing similarly powered Gamma Coupe.

Engine: Front-mounted four-cylinder horizontally opposed with belt-driven overhead camshafts and Bosch L-Jetronic fuel injection. Bore × stroke 102 × 76 mm, displacement 2484 cc. Output 105 kW (140 bhp) @ 5400 rpm, torque 208 Nm (150 lb ft) @ 3000 rpm.

Transmission: Single-disc diaphragm clutch and five-speed manual gearbox, four-speed automatic transmission optional extra. Front-wheel drive.

Suspension: Front, independent with MacPherson struts, coil springs, telescopic shock absorbers and anti-roll bar. Rear, independent with MacPherson struts, coil springs, telescopic shock absorbers and anti-roll bar.

Steering: Rack and pinion, power-assisted.

Brakes: Ventilated discs front, discs rear, servo-assisted.

Tyres: 185/70 HR–14.

Dimensions: Length 4580 mm (180.3 in), width 1730 mm (68.1 in), height 1330 mm (52.4 in), wheelbase 2670 mm (105.1 in).

Unladen weight: 1340 kg (2953 lb).

Notes: Standard equipment includes alloy wheels, electric front window lifts, front and rear head restraints, height-adjustable headlamps and tinted glass.

LANCIA (I)   Gamma Coupe 2500 Injection

Identification: Additional model to Gamma coupe range, developed from original Weber-carburettor version and supplementing similarly powered Gamma saloon.

Engine: Front-mounted four-cylinder horizontally opposed with belt-driven overhead camshafts and Bosch L-Jetronic fuel injection. Bore × stroke 102 × 76 mm, displacement 2484 cc. Output 105 kW (140 bhp) @ 5400 rpm, torque 208 Nm (150 lb ft) @ 3000 rpm.

Transmission: Single-disc diaphragm clutch and five-speed manual gearbox, four-speed automatic transmission optional extra. Front-wheel drive.

Suspension: Front, independent with MacPherson struts, coil springs, telescopic shock absorbers and anti-roll bar. Rear, independent with MacPherson struts, coil springs, telescopic shock absorbers and anti-roll bar.

Steering: Rack and pinion, power-assisted.

Brakes: Ventilated discs front, discs rear, servo-assisted.

Tyres: 185/70 HR–14

Dimensions: Length 4485 mm, (176.6 in), width 1730 mm (68.1 in), height 1330 mm (52.4 in), wheelbase 2555 mm (100.6 in).

Unladen weight: 1290 kg (2843 lb).

Notes: Standard equipment includes alloy wheels, electric window lifts, front and rear head restraints, height-adjustable headlamps and tinted glass.

LAND-ROVER (GB)   Range Rover 4-door

Identification: Four-door derivative of continuing two-door Range Rover incorporating more flexible engine and other mechanical improvements also made to two-door model.

Engine: Front-mounted V-8-cylinder with pushrod-operated overhead valves and twin Zenith-Stromberg carburettors. Bore × stroke 88.9 × 71.1 mm, displacement 3528 cc. Output 93 kW (125 bhp) @ 4000 rpm, torque 258 Nm (185 lb ft) @ 2500 rpm.

Transmission: Single-disc diaphragm clutch and four-speed manual gearbox with two-speed transfer box. Four-wheel drive.

Suspension: Front, rigid axle with coil springs, radius arms, Panhard rod and telescopic shock absorbers. Rear, rigid axle with coil springs, radius arms, A-bracket and self-levelling struts.

Steering: Recirculating ball, power-assisted.

Brakes: Discs front and rear, servo-assisted. Drum brake on rear output shaft from transfer box.

Tyres: 205–16.

Dimensions: Length 4470 mm (176 in), width 1780 mm (70 in), height 1803 mm (71 in), wheelbase 2540 mm (100 in).

Unladen weight: 1793 kg (3951 lb).

Notes: Standard equipment includes velvet-trimmed upholstery, head restraints, fully carpeted rear wheelarches, removable carpeting and rubber floor mats, radio aerial and door-mounted stereo radio speakers.

LOTUS (GB)

Identification: More powerful development of original 2-litre-engined four-seater two-door coupe incorporating aerodynamic body improvements and uprated interior trim and equipment.

Engine: Front-mounted four-cylinder in-line with twin belt-driven overhead camshafts and twin Dellorto carburettors. Bore × stroke 95.3 × 76.2 mm, displacement 2174 cc. Output 120 kW (160 bhp) @ 6500 rpm, torque 224 Nm (160 lb ft) @ 5000 rpm.

Transmission: Single-disc diaphragm clutch and five-speed manual gearbox, three-speed automatic transmission optional extra. Rear-wheel drive.

Suspension: Front, independent with wishbones, coil springs, telescopic shock absorbers and anti-roll bar. Rear, independent with trailing arms, lateral links, coil springs and telescopic shock absorbers.

Steering: Rack and pinion, power assistance optional extra.

Brakes: Discs front, drums rear, servo-assisted.

Tyres: 205/60 VR–14.

Dimensions: Length 4445 mm (175 in), width 1816 mm (71.5 in), height 1207 mm (47.5 in), wheelbase 2483 mm (97.8 in).

Unladen weight: 1102 kg (2429 lb).

Notes: Standard equipment includes alloy wheels, electric window lifts, rear screen wash/wipe, fabric upholstery, tinted glass and halogen headlamps.

LOTUS (GB)   Elite Series 2.2

Identification: More powerful development of original 2-litre-engined four-seater hatchback coupe incorporating aerodynamic body improvements and uprated interior trim and equipment.

Engine: Front-mounted four-cylinder in-line with twin belt-driven overhead camshafts and twin Dellorto carburettors. Bore × stroke 95.3 × 76.2 mm, displacement 2174 cc. Output 120 kW (160 bhp) @ 6500 rpm, torque 224 Nm (160 lb ft) @ 5000 rpm.

Transmission: Single-disc diaphragm clutch and five-speed manual gearbox, three-speed automatic transmission optional extra. Rear-wheel drive.

Suspension: Front, independent with wishbones, coil springs, telescopic shock absorbers and anti-roll bar, Rear, independent with trailing arms, lateral links, coil springs and telescopic shock absorbers.

Steering: Rack and pinion, power assistance optional extra.

Brakes: Discs front, drums rear, servo-assisted.

Tyres: 205/60 VR-14.

Dimensions: Length 4445 mm (175 in), width 1816 mm (71.5 in), height 1207 mm (47.5 in), wheelbase 2483 mm (97.8 in).

Unladen weight: 1120 kg (2468 lb).

Notes: Standard equipment includes alloy wheels, electric window lifts, rear screen wash/wipe, fabric upholstery, tinted glass and halogen headlamps.

LOTUS (GB)   Esprit Series 3

Identification: Development of Esprit Series 2.2 incorporating styling and aerodynamic changes derived from Turbo model and greater mechanical refinement.

Engine: Centrally mounted four-cylinder in-line with twin belt-driven overhead camshafts and twin Dellorto carburettors. Bore × stroke 95.3 × 76.2 mm, displacement 2174 cc. Output 120 kW (160 bhp) @ 6500 rpm, torque 224 Nm (160 lb ft) @ 5000 rpm.

Transmission: Single-disc diaphragm clutch and five-speed manual gearbox. Rear-wheel drive.

Suspension: Front, independent with wishbones, coil springs, telescopic shock absorbers and anti-roll bar. Rear, independent with trailing arms, lateral links, coil springs and telescopic shock absorbers.

Steering: Rack and pinion.

Brakes: Discs front and rear, servo-assisted.

Tyres: 205/60 VR–14 front, 205/70 VR–14 rear.

Dimensions: Length 4191 mm (165 in), width 1854 mm (73 in), height 1111 mm (43.8 in), wheelbase 2438 mm (96 in).

Unladen weight: 1020 kg (2248 lb).

Notes: Standard equipment includes alloy wheels, electric window lifts, halogen headlamps, velour upholstery, tinted glass, twin radio speakers and small-diameter padded steering wheel.

LOTUS (GB)   Turbo Esprit

Identification: Volume-production version of former limited-edition model incorporating wider-box chassis-frame, additional aerodynamic features and improved cockpit equipment.

Engine: Centrally mounted four-cylinder in-line with twin belt-driven overhead camshafts, Garrett AiResearch turbocharger and twin Dellorto carburettors. Bore × stroke 95.3 × 76.2 mm, displacement 2174 cc. Output 154 kW (210 bhp) @ 6000 rpm, torque 277 Nm (200 lb ft) @ 4000 rpm.

Transmission: Single-disc diaphragm clutch and five-speed manual gearbox. Rear-wheel drive.

Suspension: Front, independent with wishbones, coil springs, telescopic shock absorbers and anti-roll bar. Rear, independent with trailing arms, lateral links, coil springs and telescopic shock absorbers.

Steering: Rack and pinion.

Brakes: Discs front and rear, servo-assisted.

Tyres: 195/60 VR–15 front, 235/60 VR–15 rear.

Dimensions: Length 4191 mm (165 in), width 1854 mm (73 in), height 1118 mm (44 in), wheelbase 2438 mm (96 in).

Unladen weight: 1220 kg (2690 lb).

Notes: Standard equipment includes oil cooler, four radio speakers, turbo boost gauge, back-lit switch gear, English cloth upholstery and revised head restraints.

MASERATI (I)

Merak SS

Identification: Updated version of mid-engined two-seater sports coupe supplementing larger-engined two-door four-seater Maserati saloons.

Engine: Centrally mounted V-6-cylinder with twin chain-driven overhead camshafts and triple Weber carburettors. Bore × stroke 91.6 × 75 mm, displacement 2965 cc. Output 155 kW (208 bhp) @ 5800 rpm, torque 255 Nm (188 lb ft) @ 4500 rpm.

Transmission: Single-disc power-assisted diaphragm clutch and five-speed manual gearbox. Rear-wheel drive.

Suspension: Front, independent with wishbones, coil springs, telescopic shock absorbers and anti-roll bar. Rear, independent with wishbones, coil springs, telescopic shock absorbers and anti-roll bar.

Steering: Rack and pinion, power-assisted.

Brakes: Ventilated discs front and rear, power-assisted.

Tyres: 195/70 VR–15.

Dimensions: Length 4318 mm (170 in), width 1768 mm (69.6 in), height 1133 mm (44.6 in), wheelbase 2598 mm (102.3 in).

Unladen weight: 1420 kg (3130 lb).

Notes: Standard equipment includes air-conditioning, alloy wheels, electric window lifts, tinted glass, velour upholstery and limited-slip differential.

MASERATI (I)   Khamsin

Identification: Largest-engined model in Maserati range, supplementing similarly powered and 4.1-litre Kyalami coupes and 3-litre mid-engined Merak SS models.

Engine: Front-mounted V-8-cylinder with four chain-driven overhead camshafts and four Weber carburettors. Bore × stroke 94 × 89 mm, displacement 4930 cc. Output 209 kW (280 bhp) @ 5500 rpm, torque 446 Nm (323 lb ft) @ 3400 rpm.

Transmission: Single-disc power-assisted diaphragm clutch and five-speed manual gearbox. Rear-wheel drive.

Suspension: Front, independent with wishbones, coil springs, telescopic shock absorbers and anti-roll bar. Rear, independent with wishbones, coil springs, telescopic shock absorbers and anti-roll bar.

Steering: Rack and pinion, power-assisted.

Brakes: Ventilated discs front and rear, power-assisted.

Tyres: 215/70 VR–15.

Dimensions: Length 4394 mm (173 in), width 1803 mm (71 in), height 1194 mm (47 in), wheelbase 2802 mm (110.3 in).

Unladen weight: 1600 kg (3526 lb).

Notes: Standard equipment includes air-conditioning, electric window lifts, tinted glass, limited-slip differential and hydraulically operated steering, brakes and clutch.

MAZDA (J)   323 1300 3-door

Identification: Intermediate model in range of three-door hatchback saloons, bridging gap between 1.1-litre and 1.5-litre models, also available with four-door or five-door bodywork.

Engine: Front and transverse-mounted four-cylinder in-line with chain-driven overhead camshaft and Hitachi twin-choke carburettor. Bore × stroke 77 × 69.6 mm, displacement 1296 cc. Output 51 kW (68 bhp) @ 6000 rpm, torque 96 Nm (70 lb ft) @ 3500 rpm.

Transmission: Single-disc diaphragm clutch and four-speed manual gearbox. Front-wheel drive.

Suspension: Front, independent with MacPherson struts, coil springs and telescopic shock absorbers. Rear, independent with MacPherson struts, coil springs, trailing and transverse links and anti-roll bar.

Steering: Rack and pinion.

Brakes: Discs front, drums rear, servo-assisted.

Tyres: 155 SR–13.

Dimensions: Length 3955 mm (155.7 in), width 1630 mm (64.2 in), height 1375 mm (54.1 in), wheelbase 2365 mm (93.1 in).

Unladen weight: 820 kg (1807 lb).

Notes: Standard equipment includes fabric upholstery, front head restraints, interior tailgate release, radio, tinted glass, locking fuel filler cover and folding split rear seat.

MAZDA (J)

626 2000 SDX

Identification: Revised version of four-door saloon formerly known as Montrose incorporating styling and equipment changes and supplementing 1.6-litre DX model.

Engine: Front-mounted four-cylinder in-line with chain-driven overhead camshaft and Nikki carburettor. Bore × stroke 80 × 98 mm, displacement 1970 cc. Output 67 kW (90 bhp) @ 4800 rpm, torque 115 Nm (159 lb ft) @ 2500 rpm.

Transmission: Single-disc diaphragm clutch and five-speed manual gearbox, three-speed automatic transmission optional extra. Rear-wheel drive.

Suspension: Front, independent with MacPherson struts, coil springs, telescopic shock absorbers and anti-roll bar. Rear, live axle with trailing arms, Panhard rod, coil springs, telescopic shock absorbers and anti-roll bar.

Steering: Recirculating ball.

Brakes: Discs front, drums rear, servo-assisted.

Tyres: 185/70 SR–13.

Dimensions: Length 4360 mm (171.7 in), width 1660 mm (65.4 in), height 1370 mm (53.9 in), wheelbase 2510 mm (98.8 in).

Unladen weight: 1070 kg (2354 lb).

Notes: Standard equipment includes central locking, electric window lifts, fabric upholstery, halogen headlamps, radio, rev counter, adjustable head restraints and laminated screen.

113

MAZDA (J)   626 2000 SDX Coupe

Identification: Two-door coupe derivative of 2000 SDX saloon developed from Montrose models and incorporating styling and equipment changes.

Engine: Front-mounted four-cylinder in-line with chain-driven overhead camshaft and Nikki carburettor. Bore × stroke 80 × 98 mm, displacement 1970 cc. Output 67 kW (90 bhp) @ 4800 rpm, torque 115 Nm (159 lb ft) @ 2500 rpm.

Transmission: Single-disc diaphragm clutch and five-speed manual gearbox, three-speed automatic transmission optional extra. Rear-wheel drive.

Suspension: Front, independent with MacPherson struts, coil springs, telescopic shock absorbers and anti-roll bar. Rear, live axle with trailing arms, Panhard rod, coil springs, telescopic shock absorbers and anti-roll bar.

Steering: Recirculating ball.

Brakes: Discs front, drums rear, servo-assisted.

Tyres: 185/70 SR–13.

Dimensions: Length 4360 mm (171.7 in), width 1660 mm (65.4 in), height 1345 mm (53 in), wheelbase 2510 mm (98.8 in).

Unladen weight: 1070 kg (2354 lb).

Notes: Standard equipment includes central locking, electric window lifts, fabric upholstery, halogen headlamps, radio, rev counter, adjustable head restraints and laminated screen.

MAZDA (J)   RX 7

Identification: Improved-specification version of rotary-engined two-plus-two coupe incorporating many detail changes to both exterior and interior trim and higher standard of equipment.

Engine: Front-mounted twin-rotor in-line with Nikki two-stage four-barrel carburettor. Displacement 573 cc × 2, equivalence rated at 2292 cc. Output 86 kW (115 bhp) @ 6000 rpm, torque 155 Nm (112 lb ft) @ 4000 rpm.

Transmission: Single-disc diaphragm clutch and five-speed manual gearbox. Rear-wheel drive.

Suspension: Front, independent with MacPherson struts, coil springs, telescopic shock absorbers and anti-roll bar. Rear, live axle with trailing arms, coil springs, Watt linkage and anti-roll bar.

Steering: Recirculating ball.

Brakes: Discs front and rear, servo-assisted.

Tyres: 185/70 HR–13.

Dimensions: Length 4320 mm (170.1 in), width 1670 mm (65.8 in), height 1260 mm (49.6 in), wheelbase 2420 mm (95.3 in).

Unladen weight: 1050 kg (2315 lb).

Notes: Standard equipment includes rear screen wash/wipe, electrically operated window lifts and exterior mirror, alloy wheels, sliding roof, headlamp washers, cassette player and stereo radio with electric aerial.

MERCEDES-BENZ (D)

200 T

Identification: Most competitively priced model in range of five-door estates, supplementing 230 TE and 280 TE with fuel-injected petrol engines and 240 TD and 300 TD diesels.

Engine: Front-mounted four-cylinder in-line with chain-driven overhead camshaft and Stromberg carburettor. Bore × stroke 89 × 80.3 mm, displacement 1997 cc. Output 80 kW (109 bhp) @ 5200 rpm, torque 170 Nm (123 lb ft) @ 3000 rpm.

Transmission: Single-disc diaphragm clutch and four-speed manual gearbox, four-speed automatic transmission optional extra. Rear-wheel drive.

Suspension: Front, independent with wishbones, coil springs, telescopic shock absorbers and anti-roll bar. Rear, independent with trailing arms, coil springs, self-levelling struts, telescopic shock absorbers and anti-roll bar.

Steering: Recirculating ball, power-assisted.

Brakes: Discs front and rear, servo-assisted.

Tyres: 195/70 SR–14.

Dimensions: Length 4724 mm (186 in), width 1784 mm (70.2 in), height 1425 mm (56.1 in), wheelbase 2794 mm (110 in).

Unladen weight: 1455 kg (3206 lb).

Notes: Standard equipment includes central locking, rear screen wash/wipe, divided rear seat, luggage compartment roller blind and twin roof rails.

MERCEDES-BENZ (D) 230 E

Identification: Intermediate model in range of W123-series saloons incorporating new fuel-injected engine and bridging gap between 200 four-cylinder and 250 and 280 E six-cylinder models.

Engine: Front-mounted four-cylinder in-line with chain-driven overhead camshaft and Bosch fuel injection. Bore × stroke 80.3 × 95.5 mm, displacement 2299 cc. Output 101 kW (136 bhp) @ 5100 rpm, torque 205 Nm (151 lb ft) @ 3500 rpm.

Transmission: Single-disc diaphragm clutch and five-speed manual gearbox, four-speed automatic transmission optional extra. Rear-wheel drive.

Suspension: Front, independent with wishbones, coil springs, telescopic shock absorbers and anti-roll bar. Rear, independent with trailing arms, coil springs, telescopic shock absorbers and anti-roll bar.

Steering: Recirculating ball, power-assisted.

Brakes: Discs front and rear, servo-assisted.

Tyres: 175 HR–14.

Dimensions: Length 4725 mm (186 in), width 1786 mm (70.3 in), height 1438 mm (56.6 in), wheelbase 2795 mm (110 in).

Unladen weight: 1360 kg (2997 lb).

Notes: Standard equipment includes central locking, front head restraints, headlamp height adjustment, tool kit and height-adjustable driver's seat.

MERCEDES-BENZ (D)   280 CE

Identification: Improved version of top model in range of W123 series of two-door four-seater coupes, supplementing 230 CE model and incorporating improvements in fuel efficiency.

Engine: Front-mounted six-cylinder in-line with twin chain-driven overhead camshafts and Bosch fuel injection. Bore × stroke 86 × 78.8 mm, displacement 2746 cc. Output 136 kW (185 bhp) @ 5800 rpm, torque 245 Nm (177 lb ft) @ 4500 rpm.

Transmission: Single-disc diaphragm clutch and five-speed manual gearbox or four-speed automatic transmission. Rear-wheel drive.

Suspension: Front, independent with wishbones, coil springs, gas-filled telescopic shock absorbers and anti-roll bar. Rear, independent with trailing arms, coil springs, gas-filled telescopic shock absorbers and anti-roll bar.

Steering: Recirculating ball, power-assisted.

Brakes: Discs front and rear, servo-assisted.

Tyres: 195/70 HR–14.

Dimensions: Length 4640 mm (182.7 in), width 1786 mm (70.3 in), height 1395 mm (54.9 in), wheelbase 2710 mm (106.7 in).

Unladen weight: 1450 kg (3197 lb).

Notes: Standard equipment includes tinted glass, fabric upholstery, head restraints, first-aid kit, halogen headlamps, electric window lifts and central locking.

MERCEDES-BENZ (D)   280 SL

Identification: Smallest-engined of three two-seater sports-touring cars, supplementing V-8-engined 380 SL and 500 SL models.

Engine: Front-mounted six-cylinder in-line with twin chain-driven overhead camshafts and Bosch K-Jetronic fuel injection. Bore × stroke 86 × 78.8 mm, displacement 2746 cc. Output 136 kW (185 bhp) @ 5800 rpm, torque 245 Nm (177 lb ft) @ 4500 rpm.

Transmission: Single-disc diaphragm clutch and five-speed manual gearbox or four-speed automatic transmission. Rear-wheel drive.

Suspension: Front, independent with wishbones, coil springs, telescopic shock absorbers and anti-roll bar. Rear, independent with trailing arms, coil springs, telescopic shock absorbers and anti-roll bar.

Steering: Recirculating ball, power-assisted.

Brakes: Discs front and rear, servo-assisted.

Tyres: 195/70 HR–14.

Dimensions: Length 4390 mm (172.8 in), width 1790 mm (70.5 in), height 1300 mm (51.2 in), wheelbase 2460 mm (96.9 in).

Unladen weight: 1500 kg (3305 lb).

Notes: Standard equipment includes reclining seats, head restraints, central locking, door mirrors and rev counter.

MERCEDES-BENZ (D) 380 SEL

Identification: Longer-wheelbase version of the 380 SE four-door saloon offering increased rear-passenger leg room, also available with 5-litre engine as 500 SEL.

Engine: Front-mounted V-8-cylinder with chain-driven overhead camshafts and Bosch mechanical fuel injection. Bore × stroke 88 × 78.9 mm, displacement 3839 cc. Output 150 kW (201 bhp) @ 5250 rpm, torque 321 Nm (232 lb ft) @ 3250 rpm.

Transmission: Four-speed automatic transmission. Rear-wheel drive.

Suspension: Front, independent with wishbones, coil springs, telescopic shock absorbers and anti-roll bar. Rear, independent with trailing arms, coil springs, telescopic shock absorbers and anti-roll bar.

Steering: Recirculating ball, power-assisted.

Brakes: Discs front and rear, servo-assisted.

Tyres: 205/70 VR–14.

Dimensions: Length 5135 mm (202.2 in), width 1820 mm (71.7 in), height 1440 mm (56.7 in), wheelbase 3075 mm (121.1 in).

Unladen weight: 1640 kg (3564 lb).

Notes: Standard equipment includes tinted glass, headlamp wash/wipe, electric window lifts, central locking, fabric upholstery and height-adjustable seat belts.

MERCEDES-BENZ (D)   500 SE

Identification: Most powerful model in latest S-series of four-door saloons in standard-wheelbase form, supplementing similarly bodied 2.8-litre and 3.8-litre models.

Engine: Front-mounted V-8-cylinder with chain-driven overhead camshafts and Bosch mechanical fuel injection. Bore × stroke 96.5 × 85 mm, displacement 4973 cc. Output 171 kW (228 bhp) @ 4750 rpm, torque 413 Nm (299 lb ft) @ 3200 rpm.

Transmission: Four-speed automatic transmission. Rear-wheel drive.

Suspension: Front, independent with wishbones, coil springs, telescopic shock absorbers and anti-roll bar. Rear, independent with trailing arms, coil springs, telescopic shock absorbers and anti-roll bar.

Steering: Recirculating ball, power-assisted.

Brakes: Discs front and rear, servo-assisted.

Tyres: 205/70 VR–14.

Dimensions: Length 4995 mm (196.7 in), width 1820 mm (71.7 in), height 1436 mm (56.6 in), wheelbase 2935 mm (115.6 in).

Unladen weight: 1645 kg (3580 lb).

Notes: Standard equipment includes air-conditioning, anti-lock braking, cruise control, limited-slip differential, electric window lifts, central locking, velour upholstery, headlamp wash/wipe and tinted glass.

MERCEDES-BENZ (D)   380 SEC

Identification: Smaller-engined of two two-door coupes based on shorter-wheelbase version of S-series saloon chassis and replacing similarly powered 380 SLC coupe.

Engine: Front-mounted V-8-cylinder with chain-driven overhead camshafts and Bosch mechanical fuel injection. Bore × stroke 88 × 78.9 mm, displacement 3839 cc. Output 150 kW (201 bhp) @ 5250 rpm, torque 321 Nm (232 lb ft) @ 3250 rpm.

Transmission: Four-speed automatic transmission. Rear-wheel drive.

Suspension: Front, independent with wishbones, coil springs, telescopic shock absorbers and anti-roll bar. Rear, independent with trailing arms, coil springs, telescopic shock absorbers and anti-roll bar.

Steering: Recirculating ball, power-assisted.

Brakes: Discs front and rear, servo-assisted.

Tyres: 205/70 VR–14.

Dimensions: Length 4910 mm (193.3 in) width 1828 mm (72 in), height 1406 mm (55.4 in), wheelbase 2850 mm (112.2 in).

Unladen weight: 1585 kg (3493 lb).

Notes: Standard equipment includes velour or leather upholstery central locking, electric window lifts, electrically positioned seat belts and concealed screen wipers.

MERCEDES-BENZ (D)   500 SEC

Identification: Larger-engined of two two-door coupes based on shorter-wheelbase version of S-series saloon chassis, supplementing 380 SEC model.

Engine: Front-mounted V-8-cylinder with chain-driven overhead camshafts and Bosch mechanical fuel injection. Bore × stroke 96.5 × 85 mm, displacement 4973 cc. Output 170 kW (228 bhp) @ 4750 rpm, torque 413 Nm (299 lb ft) @ 3000 rpm.

Transmission: Four-speed automatic transmission. Rear-wheel drive.

Suspension: Front, independent with wishbones, coil springs, telescopic shock absorbers and anti-roll bar. Rear, independent with trailing arms, coil springs, telescopic shock absorbers and anti-roll bar.

Steering: Recirculating ball, power-assisted.

Brakes: Discs front and rear, servo-assisted.

Tyres: 205/70 VR–14.

Dimensions: Length 4910 mm (193.3 in), width 1828 mm (72 in), height 1406 mm (55.4 in), wheelbase 2845 mm (112 in).

Unladen weight: 1610 kg (3548 lb).

Notes: Standard equipment includes velour or leather upholstery, central locking, electric window lifts, electrically positioned seat belts and concealed screen wipers.

MORRIS (GB)   Ital 1.7 HLS

Identification: Intermediate-engined top-specification version of Ital saloon range, supplementing 1.3-litre and 2-litre models and L and HL trim and equipment levels.

Engine: Front-mounted four-cylinder in-line with belt-driven overhead camshaft and SU carburettor. Bore × stroke 84.5 × 75.8 mm, displacement 1698 cc. Output 58 kW (78 bhp) @ 5150 rpm, torque 129 Nm (93 lb ft) @ 3480 rpm.

Transmission: Single-disc diaphragm clutch and four-speed manual gearbox. Rear-wheel drive.

Suspension: Front, independent with wishbones, torsion bars, lever-type shock absorbers and anti-roll bar. Rear, live axle with semi-elliptic springs, telescopic shock absorbers and anti-roll bar.

Steering: Rack and pinion.

Brakes: Discs front, drums rear, servo-assisted.

Tyres: 155 SR–13.

Dimensions: Length 4343 mm (171 in), width 1636 mm (64.4 in), height 1418 mm (55.8 in), wheelbase 2438 mm (96 in).

Unladen weight: 950 kg (2094 lb).

Notes: Standard equipment includes fabric upholstery, vinyl roof, tinted glass, radio, halogen headlamps and rev counter.

OPEL (D)   Kadett 1.3 Hatch 3-door

Identification: Intermediate model in range of two, three, four and five-door saloons with choice of 1.2-litre or 1.3-litre engines.

Engine: Front and transverse-mounted four-cylinder in-line with belt-driven overhead camshaft and Solex carburettor. Bore × stroke 75 × 73.4 mm, displacement 1297 cc. Output 45 kW (60 bhp) @ 5800 rpm, torque 94 Nm (69 lb ft) @ 3400 rpm.

Transmission: Single-disc diaphragm clutch and four-speed manual gearbox. Front-wheel drive.

Suspension: Front, independent with MacPherson struts, coil springs, telescopic shock absorbers and anti-roll bar. Rear, dead axle with trailing arms, coil springs, telescopic shock absorbers and anti-roll bar.

Steering: Rack and pinion.

Brakes: Discs front, drums rear, servo-assisted.

Tyres: 155 SR–13.

Dimensions: Length 4000 mm (157.5 in), width 1640 mm (64.6 in), height 1380 mm (54.3 in), wheelbase 2515 mm (99 in).

Unladen weight: 835 kg (1837 lb).

Notes: Standard equipment includes rear screen wash/wipe, fabric upholstery, head restraints and front and rear roof spoilers.

OPEL (D)

Identification: Sporting model of Kadett range incorporating uprated suspension, wheels and tyres and additional front and rear spoilers.

Engine: Front and transverse-mounted four-cylinder in-line with belt-driven overhead camshaft and GM carburettor. Bore × stroke 75 × 73.4 mm, displacement 1297 cc. Output 55 kW (74 bhp) @ 5800 rpm, torque 101 Nm (73 lb ft) @ 3800 rpm.

Transmission: Single-disc diaphragm clutch and four-speed manual gearbox. Front-wheel drive.

Suspension: Front, independent with MacPherson struts, coil springs, telescopic shock absorbers and anti-roll bar. Rear, dead axle with trailing arms, coil springs, telescopic shock absorbers and anti-roll bar.

Steering: Rack and pinion.

Brakes: Discs front, drums rear, servo-assisted.

Tyres: 185/60 SR–14.

Dimensions: Length 4000 mm (157.5 in), width 1650 mm (65 in), height 1397 mm (55 in), wheelbase 2515 mm (99 in).

Unladen weight: 855 kg (1885 lb).

Notes: Standard equipment includes alloy wheels, Recaro front seats, rear screen wash/wipe, full instrumentation and tool kit.

OPEL (D)   Kadett Voyage Berlina 1.6

Identification: Top-specification estate car model in Kadett range, supplementing three, four and five-door saloons with choice of 1.2 and 1.3-litre engines.

Engine: Front and transverse-mounted four-cylinder in-line with belt-driven overhead camshaft and GM carburettor. Bore × stroke 80 × 79.5 mm, displacement 1598 cc. Output 67 kW (90 bhp) @ 5800 rpm, torque 129 Nm (93 lb ft) @ 3800 rpm.

Transmission: Single-disc diaphragm clutch and four-speed manual gearbox. Front-wheel drive.

Suspension: Front, independent with MacPherson struts, coil springs, telescopic shock absorbers and anti-roll bar. Rear, dead axle with trailing arms, coil springs, telescopic shock absorbers and anti-roll bar.

Steering: Rack and pinion.

Brakes: Discs front, drums rear, servo-assisted.

Tyres: 165 SR–13.

Dimensions: Length 4210 mm (165.7 in), width 1638 mm (64.5 in), height 1400 mm (55.1 in), wheelbase 2515 mm (99 in).

Unladen weight: 925 kg (2039 lb).

Notes: Standard equipment includes velour upholstery, head restraints, rear screen wash/wipe, centre console and full instrumentation including fuel consumption meter.

OPEL (D)

Ascona Berlina 1.6

Identification: Intermediate model in new front-drive range of Ascona saloons and hatches, equivalent in Vauxhall range to Cavalier L 1600 but also available with 1.3-litre engine.

Engine: Front and transverse-mounted four-cylinder in-line with belt-driven overhead camshaft and GM carburettor. Bore × stroke 80 × 79.5 mm, displacement 1598 cc. Output 67 kW (90 bhp) @ 5800 rpm, torque 129 Nm (93 lb ft) @ 3800 rpm.

Transmission: Single-disc diaphragm clutch and four-speed manual gearbox. Front-wheel drive.

Suspension: Front, independent with MacPherson struts, coil springs, telescopic shock absorbers and anti-roll bar. Rear, semi-independent with trailing arms, torsion beam, coil springs, telescopic shock absorbers and anti-roll bar.

Steering: Rack and pinion.

Brakes: Discs front, drums rear, servo-assisted.

Tyres: 165 SR–13.

Dimensions: Length 4366 mm (171.9 in), width 1668 mm (65.7 in), height 1395 mm (54.9 in), wheelbase 2574 mm (101.3 in).

Unladen weight: 1010 kg (2227 lb).

Notes: Standard equipment includes fabric upholstery, head restraints, centre console, carpeted luggage compartment, locking fuel filler cap and internally adjustable rear-view mirror.

OPEL (D)   Rekord Berlina CD

Identification: Top model in Rekord range of medium-size saloons and estate cars with choice of 2-litre petrol and 2.3-litre diesel engine and two trim levels.

Engine: Front-mounted four-cylinder in-line with chain-driven overhead camshaft and GM carburettor. Bore × stroke 95 × 69.8 mm, displacement 1979 cc. Output 74 kW (100 bhp) @ 5400 rpm, torque 148 Nm (107 lb ft) @ 3800 rpm.

Transmission: Single-disc diaphragm clutch and four-speed manual gearbox, three-speed automatic transmission optional extra. Rear-wheel drive.

Suspension: Front, independent with wishbones, coil springs, telescopic shock absorbers and anti-roll bar. Rear, live axle with trailing and lateral arms, coil springs and telescopic shock absorbers.

Steering: Rack and pinion, power assistance optional extra.

Brakes: Discs front, drums rear, servo-assisted.

Tyres: 175 SR-14.

Dimensions: Length 4742 mm (186.7 in), width 1726 mm (68 in), height 1361 mm (53.6 in), wheelbase 2667 mm (105 in).

Unladen weight: 1130 kg (2491 lb).

Notes: Standard equipment includes velour upholstery, head restraints, height-adjustable driver's seat, adjustable instrument illumination, carpeted luggage compartment and fuel consumption meter.

OPEL (D)   Commodore Berlina

Identification: Standard version of intermediate four-door saloon bridging gap between Rekord and Senator saloons and based on Rekord bodyshell, also available in higher-specificaton CD form.

Engine: Front-mounted six-cylinder in-line with chain-driven overhead camshaft and Zenith carburettor. Bore × stroke 87 × 69.8 mm, displacement 2490 cc. Output 85 kW (115 bhp) @ 5200 rpm, torque 179 Nm (132 lb ft) @ 3800 rpm.

Transmission: Single-disc diaphragm clutch and four-speed manual gearbox, five-speed overdrive gearbox or three-speed automatic transmission optional extra. Rear-wheel drive.

Suspension: Front, independent with MacPherson struts, coil springs, telescopic shock absorbers and anti-roll bar. Rear, live axle with four-link system, coil springs, telescopic shock absorbers and anti-roll bar.

Steering: Recirculating ball, power-assisted.

Brakes: Discs front, drums rear, servo-assisted.

Tyres: 195/70 HR-14.

Dimensions: Length 4732 mm (186.3 in), width 1722 mm (67.8 in), height 1410 mm (55.5 in), wheelbase 2667 mm (105 in).

Unladen weight: 1220 kg (2690 lb).

Notes: Standard equipment includes velour upholstery, head restraints, halogen headlamps, fuel consumption meter and colour-co-ordinated upholstery and body trim.

OPEL (D)   Senator CD

Identification: Top model in largest Opel saloon range, supplementing Monza coupe with similar mechanical specification and also available with 2.5 or 3-litre carburettor-equipped engine.

Engine: Front-mounted six-cylinder in-line with chain-driven overhead camshaft and Bosch L-Jetronic fuel injection. Bore × stroke 95 × 69.8 mm, displacement 2968 cc. Output 135 kW (180 bhp) @ 5800 rpm, torque 253 Nm (183 lb ft) @ 4200 rpm.

Transmission: Three-speed automatic transmission. Rear-wheel drive.

Suspension: Front, independent with MacPherson struts, coil springs, telescopic shock absorbers and anti-roll bar. Rear, independent with trailing arms, coil springs, telescopic shock absorbers and anti-roll bar.

Steering: Recirculating ball, power-assisted.

Brakes: Ventilated discs front, discs rear, servo-assisted.

Tyres: 195/70 HR-14.

Dimensions: Length 4877 mm (192 in), width 1726 mm (68 in), height 1366 mm (53.8 in), wheelbase 2683 mm (105.6 in).

Unladen weight: 1370 kg (3020 lb).

Notes: Standard equipment includes velour upholstery, head restraints, central locking, electric window lifts, alloy wheels, tinted glass and sliding roof.

Identification: High-performance saloon model in 104 range featuring 1.4-litre engine also used in 104 ZS three-door hatchback coupe version.

Engine: Front and transverse-mounted four-cylinder in-line with chain-driven overhead camshaft and Solex carburettor. Bore × stroke 75 × 77 mm, displacement 1360 cc. Output 54 kW (72 bhp) @ 6000 rpm, torque 109 Nm (79 lb ft) @ 3000 rpm.

Transmission: Single-disc diaphragm clutch and four-speed manual gearbox. Front-wheel drive.

Suspension: Front, independent with MacPherson struts, coil springs, telescopic shock absorbers and anti-roll bar. Rear, independent with trailing arms, coil springs, telescopic shock absorbers and anti-roll bar.

Steering: Rack and pinion.

Brakes: Discs front, drums rear, servo-assisted.

Tyres: 165/70 SR–13.

Dimensions: Length 3617 mm (142.4 in), width 1521 mm (59.9 in), height 1407 mm (55.4 in), wheelbase 2420 mm (95.3 in).

Unladen weight: 825 kg (1815 lb)

Notes: Standard equipment includes alloy wheels, fabric upholstery, tinted glass, electric front window lifts and head restraints.

PEUGEOT (F)   305 S

Identification: High-performance model at top end of 305 range combining more powerful version of 1.5-litre engine with high level of equipment.

Engine: Front and transverse-mounted four-cylinder in-line with chain-driven overhead camshaft and twin-choke Solex carburettor. Bore × stroke 78 × 77 mm, displacement 1472 cc. Output 67 kW (89 bhp) @ 6000 rpm, torque 127 Nm (92 lb ft) @ 3000 rpm.

Transmission: Single-disc diaphragm clutch and four-speed manual gearbox. Front-wheel drive.

Suspension: Front, independent with MacPherson struts, coil springs, telescopic shock absorbers and anti-roll bar. Rear, independent with trailing arms, coil springs, telescopic shock absorbers and anti-roll bar.

Steering: Rack and pinion.

Brakes: Discs front, drums rear, servo-assisted.

Tyres: 165/70 SR-14.

Dimensions: Length 4237 mm (166.8 in), width 1640 mm (64.6 in), height 1405 mm (55.3 in), wheelbase 2620 mm (103.2 in).

Unladen weight: 965 kg (2127 lb).

Notes: Standard equipment includes central locking, sliding roof, electric front window lifts, tinted glass, halogen headlamps, rev counter, tweed upholstery and internally adjustable door mirror.

PEUGEOT (F)

Identification: Top model in revised range of 505 four-door saloons supplementing carburettor-equipped 2-litre SR and GR models and 2.5-litre GRD diesel version.

Engine: Front-mounted four-cylinder in-line with belt-driven overhead camshaft and Bosch K-Jetronic fuel injection. Bore × stroke 88 × 82 mm, displacement 1995 cc. Output 79 kW (110 bhp) @ 5250 rpm, torque 171 Nm (124 lb ft) @ 4000 rpm.

Transmission: Single-disc diaphragm clutch and five-speed manual gearbox, three-speed automatic transmission optional extra. Rear-wheel drive.

Suspension: Front, independent with MacPherson struts, coil springs, telescopic shock absorbers and anti-roll bar. Rear, independent with trailing arms, coil springs, telescopic shock absorbers and anti-roll bar.

Steering: Rack and pinion, power-assisted.

Brakes: Discs front and rear, servo-assisted.

Tyres: 175 HR–14.

Dimensions: Length 4500 mm (180.3 in), width 1720 mm (67.7 in), height 1450 mm (57.1 in), wheelbase 2740 mm (107.0 in)

Unladen weight: 1210 kg (2667 lb).

Notes: Standard equipment includes velour upholstery, head restraints, electric sliding roof and window lifts, central locking, tinted glass, stereo radio/cassette player and digital clock.

PEUGEOT (F)   604 TI

Identification: Top model in 604 range of four-door saloons, supplementing carburettor-equipped 604 SL petrol-engined and 604D Turbo diesel-engined models.

Engine: Front-mounted V-6-cylinder with chain-driven overhead camshafts and Bosch K-Jetronic fuel injection. Bore × stroke 88 × 73 mm, displacement 2664 cc. Output 108 kW (144 bhp) @ 5500 rpm, torque 220 Nm (159 lb ft) @ 3000 rpm.

Transmission: Single-disc diaphragm clutch and five-speed manual gearbox, three-speed automatic transmission optional extra. Rear-wheel drive.

Suspension: Front, independent with MacPherson struts, coil springs, telescopic shock absorbers and anti-roll bar. Rear, independent with trailing arms, coil springs, telescopic shock absorbers and anti-roll bar.

Steering: Rack and pinion, power-assisted.

Brakes: Discs front and rear, servo-assisted.

Tyres: 195/65 HR–390.

Dimensions: Length 4720 mm (185.8 in), width 1770 mm (69.7 in), height 1430 mm (56.3 in), wheelbase 2802 mm (110.3 in).

Unladen weight: 1475 kg (3251 lb).

Notes: Standard equipment includes velour or leather upholstery, head restraints, alloy wheels, electric window lifts, sliding roof and tinted glass.

Identification: Addition to Porsche range derived from 924 series but combining new 2½-litre engine and bodywork first seen on 924 Carrera GT model.

Engine: Front-mounted four-cylinder in-line with belt-driven overhead camshaft and Bosch L-Jetronic fuel injection. Bore × stroke 100 × 78.9 mm, displacement 2479 cc. Output 122 kW (163 bhp) @ 5800 rpm, torque 209 Nm (151 lb ft) @ 3000 rpm.

Transmission: Single-disc diaphragm clutch and rear-mounted five-speed manual gearbox, three-speed automatic transmission optional extra. Rear-wheel drive.

Suspension: Front, independent with MacPherson struts, coil springs, telescopic shock absorbers and anti-roll bar. Rear, independent with trailing arms, torsion bars, telescopic shock absorbers and anti-roll bar.

Steering: Rack and pinion.

Brakes: Ventilated discs front and rear, servo-assisted.

Tyres: 185/70 VR-15.

Dimensions: Length 4200 mm (165.4 in), width 1735 mm (68.3 in), height 1275 mm (50.2 in), wheelbase 2400 mm (94.5 in).

Unladen weight: 1180 kg (2601 lb).

Notes: Standard equipment includes electric window lifts, front and rear spoilers, rear screen wash/wipe, stereo radio/cassette player and tinted glass.

PORSCHE (D)

928S

Identification: Improved version of flagship of Porsche range, supplementing 928 model and incorporating revised fresh-air ventilation and seat-adjustment arrangements.

Engine: Front-mounted V-8-cylinder with single belt-driven overhead camshafts and Bosch K-Jetronic fuel injection. Bore × stroke 97 × 78.9 mm, displacement 4664 cc. Output 224 kW (300 bhp) @ 5900 rpm, torque 440 Nm (318 lb ft) @ 4500 rpm.

Transmission: Single-disc diaphragm clutch and five-speed manual gearbox or three-speed automatic transmission. Rear-wheel drive.

Suspension: Front, independent with wishbones, coil springs, telescopic shock absorbers and anti-roll bar. Rear, independent with trailing and transverse arms, coil springs, telescopic shock absorbers and transverse torsion bars.

Steering: Rack and pinion, power-assisted.

Brakes: Ventilated discs front and rear, servo-assisted.

Tyres: 225/50 VR–16.

Dimensions: Length 4448 mm (175.1 in), width 1836 mm (72.3 in), height 1313 mm (51.7 in), wheelbase 2500 mm (98.4 in).

Unladen weight: 1450 kg (3196 lb).

Notes: Standard equipment includes air-conditioning, leather upholstery, electrically adjustable seats and forged alloy wheels.

PRINCESS (GB)

1.7 HLS

Identification: Improved version of smallest-engined model in Princess range, supplementing L and HL versions and offering more economical alternative to 2.0 and 2.2-litre models.

Engine: Front and transverse-mounted four-cylinder in-line with belt-driven overhead camshaft and SU carburettor. Bore × stroke 84.5 × 75.8 mm, displacement 1695 cc. Output 65 kW (87 bhp) @ 5200 rpm, torque 134 Nm (97 lb ft) @ 3800 rpm.

Transmission: Single-disc diaphragm clutch and four-speed manual gearbox, three-speed automatic transmission optional extra. Front-wheel drive.

Suspension: Front, independent with wishbones, Hydragas spring units and integral shock absorbers. Rear, independent with trailing arms, Hydragas spring units (linked to front units) and integral shock absorbers.

Steering: Rack and pinion, power-assisted.

Brakes: Discs front, drums rear, servo-assisted.

Tyres: 185/70 SR–14.

Dimensions: Length 4455 mm (175.4 in), width 1730 mm (68.1 in), height 1410 mm (55.5 in), wheelbase 2673 mm (105.3 in).

Unladen weight: 1150 kg (2535 lb).

Notes: Standard equipment includes radio/cassette player, velour upholstery, tinted glass, carpeted luggage compartment and vinyl trimmed rear quarter panels.

RAPPORT (GB)

Ritz

Identification: High-specification four-door saloon based on Honda Accord body structure, engine and running gear and incorporating extensive aerodynamic changes.

Engine: Front and transverse-mounted four-cylinder in-line with belt-driven overhead camshaft and Keihin carburettor. Bore × stroke 77 × 86 mm, displacement 1602 cc. Output 59 kW (80 bhp) @ 5300 rpm, torque 127 Nm (93 lb ft) @ 3500 rpm.

Transmission: Two-speed semi-automatic transmission with electric overdrive. Front-wheel drive.

Suspension: Front, independent with MacPherson struts, coil springs, telescopic shock absorbers and anti-roll bar. Rear, independent with MacPherson struts, coil springs, radius arms, telescopic shock absorbers and anti-roll bar.

Steering: Rack and pinion, power-assisted.

Brakes: Discs front, drums rear, servo-assisted.

Tyres: 155 SR–13.

Dimensions: Length 4345 mm (171 in), width 1620 mm (63.8 in), height 1360 mm (53.5 in), wheelbase 2380 mm (93.7 in).

Unladen weight: 1180 kg (2602 lb).

Notes: Standard equipment includes leather and Dralon upholstery and trim, walnut cappings, air-conditioning, electrically controlled aerofoil, electric window lifts, radio/cassette player and electric aerial.

RELIANT (GB)   Scimitar GTC

Identification: Hardtop version of convertible derivative of Scimitar GTE hatchback incorporating fixed roll-over hoop; convertible hood remains concealed on car for use when hardtop is removed.

Engine: Front-mounted V-6-cylinder with pushrod-operated overhead valves and Weber carburettor. Bore × stroke 93 × 68.5 mm, displacement 2792 cc. Output 101 kW (135 bhp) @ 5200 rpm, torque 220 Nm (159 lb ft) @ 3000 rpm.

Transmission: Single-disc diaphragm clutch and four-speed manual gearbox with overdrive on 3rd and 4th, three-speed automatic transmission optional extra. Rear-wheel drive.

Suspension: Front, independent with wishbones, coil springs, telescopic shock absorbers and anti-roll bar. Rear, live axle with trailing arms, Watt linkage, coil springs and telescopic shock absorbers.

Steering: Rack and pinion, power-assistance optional extra.

Brakes: Discs front, drums rear, servo-assisted.

Tyres: 185 HR–14.

Dimensions: Length 4432 mm (174.5 in), width 1720 mm (67.8 in), height 1321 mm (52 in), wheelbase 2637 mm (103.8 in).

Unladen weight: 1296 kg (2856 lb).

Notes: Standard equipment includes hood stowage cover, individually folding rear seats, front head restraints, dual head-lamps, velour-faced upholstery and twin-speaker radio.

RENAULT (F)

5 Auto 1400

Identification: Larger-engined derivative of former 1.3-litre five-door Renault 5, also available with three-door body and using engine also available in 63-bhp form in certain 18 and Fuego models.

Engine: Front-mounted four-cylinder in-line with pushrod-operated overhead valves and Solex carburettor. Bore × stroke 76 × 77 mm, displacement 1397 cc. Output 44 kW (59 bhp) @ 5500 rpm, torque 101 Nm (73 lb ft) @ 3000 rpm.

Transmission: Three-speed automatic transmission. Front-wheel drive.

Suspension: Front, independent with wishbones, torsion bars, telescopic shock absorbers and anti-roll bar. Rear, independent with trailing arms, torsion bars and telescopic shock absorbers.

Steering: Rack and pinion.

Brakes: Discs front, drums rear, servo-assisted.

Tyres: 145 SR–13.

Dimensions: Length 3530 mm (139 in), width 1525 mm (60 in), height 1395 mm (54.9 in), wheelbase 2434 mm (95.8 in) left side, 2404 mm (94.7 in) right side.

Unladen weight: 810 kg (1786 lb).

Notes: Standard equipment includes fabric upholstery, head restraints, folding rear seat, body side protection panels and rear screen wash/wipe.

Identification: Base model in multi-model range of 1.1 and 1.4-litre four-door saloons, also available with similar engine in TC, GTC and TCE versions.

Engine: Front and transverse-mounted four-cylinder in-line with pushrod-operated overhead valves and Zenith carburettor. Bore × stroke 70 × 72 mm, displacement 1108 cc. Output 36 kW (48 bhp) @ 5250 rpm, torque 79 Nm (59 lb ft) @ 2500 rpm.

Transmission: Single-disc diaphragm clutch and four-speed manual gearbox. Front-wheel drive.

Suspension: Front, independent with MacPherson struts, coil springs, telescopic shock absorbers and anti-roll bar. Rear, independent with trailing arms, transverse torsion bars, telescopic shock absorbers and anti-roll bar.

Steering: Rack and pinion.

Brakes: Discs front, drums rear, servo-assisted.

Tyres: 145 SR–13.

Dimensions: Length 4063 mm (160 in), width 1634 mm (64.3 in), height 1330 mm (52.4 in), wheelbase 2477 mm (97.5 in).

Unladen weight: 805 kg (1775 lb).

Notes: Standard equipment includes centre console, dashboard coin slot, fabric upholstery, two-speed wipers with flick-wipe and electric screen wash.

RENAULT (F)

9 GTS

Identification: High-specification model in multi-car Renault 9 range with most powerful of three versions of 1.4-litre engine also offered with TS and TSE models.

Engine: Front and transverse-mounted four-cylinder in-line with pushrod-operated overhead valves and Weber twin-choke carburettor. Bore × stroke 76 × 77 mm, displacement 1397 cc. Output 52 kW (72 bhp) @ 5750 rpm, torque 104 Nm (78 lb ft) @ 3500 rpm.

Transmission: Single-disc diaphragm clutch and five-speed manual gearbox. Front-wheel drive.

Suspension: Front, independent with MacPherson struts, coil springs, telescopic shock absorbers and anti-roll bar. Rear, independent with trailing arms, transverse torsion bars, telescopic shock absorbers and anti-roll bar.

Steering: Rack and pinion.

Brakes: Discs front, drums rear, servo-assisted.

Tyres: 155 SR–13.

Dimensions: Length 4063 mm (160 in), width 1634 mm (64.3 in), height 1330 mm (52.4 in), wheelbase 2477 mm (97.5 in).

Unladen weight: 845 kg (1863 lb).

Notes: Standard equipment includes velour upholstery, locking fuel filler cap, rear spoiler, front head restraints, intermittent screen wipe and sports-type steering wheel.

RENAULT (F)   Fuego GTX

Identification: Top model in range of Fuego hatchback coupes embracing 1.4-litre, 1.6-litre and 2-litre engines and supplementing TL, GTL and GTS versions.

Engine: Front-mounted four-cylinder in-line with belt-driven overhead camshaft and Weber carburettor. Bore × stroke 88 × 82 mm, displacement 1995 cc. Output 82 kW (110 bhp) @ 5500 rpm, torque 166 Nm (120 lb ft) @ 3000 rpm.

Transmission: Single-disc diaphragm clutch and five-speed manual gearbox. Front-wheel drive.

Suspension: Front, independent with wishbones, coil springs, telescopic shock absorbers and anti-roll bar. Rear, dead axle with trailing arms, coil springs, telescopic shock absorbers and anti-roll bar.

Steering: Rack and pinion, power-assisted.

Brakes: Discs front, drums rear, servo-assisted.

Tyres: 185/65 HR–14.

Dimensions: Length 4360 mm (171.6 in), width 1690 mm (66.5 in), height 1315 mm (51.8 in), wheelbase 2445 mm (96.3 in).

Unladen weight: 1080 kg (2377 lb).

Notes: Standard equipment includes individually folding rear seats, removable luggage cover, alloy wheels, head restraints, halogen headlamps, electric window lifts and rear screen wash/wipe.

RENAULT (F) 18 GTL

Identification: Larger-engined derivative of model formerly fitted with 1.4-litre engine, also available as five-door estate car and equipped with five-speed transmission.

Engine: Front-mounted four-cylinder in-line with pushrod-operated overhead valves and Solex carburettor. Bore × stroke 79 × 84 mm, displacement 1647 cc. Output 55 kW (74 bhp) @ 5500 rpm, torque 106 Nm (77 lb ft) @ 3500 rpm.

Transmission: Single-disc diaphragm clutch and five-speed manual gearbox. Front-wheel drive.

Suspension: Front, independent with wishbones, coil springs, telescopic shock absorbers and anti-roll bar. Rear, dead axle with trailing arms, coil springs, telescopic shock absorbers and anti-roll bar.

Steering: Rack and pinion.

Brakes: Discs front, drums rear, servo-assisted.

Tyres: 155 SR–13.

Dimensions: Length 4380 mm (172.5 in), width 1690 mm (66.5 in), height 1405 mm (55.3 in), wheelbase 2440 mm (96.1 in).

Unladen weight: 960 kg (2116 lb).

Notes: Standard equipment includes fabric upholstery, head restraints, centre console, halogen headlamps, headlamp wash/wipe and laminated screen.

RENAULT (F)

18 GTD

Identification: More fully equipped of two diesel-engined derivatives of petrol-engined 18 saloons, supplementing TD saloon and estate with similar engine.

Engine: Front-mounted four-cylinder in-line with belt-driven overhead camshaft and Bosch diesel injection. Bore × stroke 86 × 89 mm, displacement 2068 cc. Output 48 kW (66.5 bhp) @ 4500 rpm, torque 129 Nm (93 lb ft) @ 2250 rpm.

Transmission: Single-disc diaphragm clutch and five-speed manual gearbox. Front-wheel drive.

Suspension: Front, independent with wishbones, coil springs, telescopic shock absorbers and anti-roll bar. Rear, dead axle with trailing arms, coil springs, telescopic shock absorbers and anti-roll bar.

Steering: Rack and pinion, power assistance optional extra.

Brakes: Discs front, drums rear, servo-assisted.

Tyres: 165 SR–13.

Dimensions: Length 4381 mm (172.5 in), width 1689 mm (66.5 in), height 1405 mm (55.3 in), wheelbase 2400 mm (96 in).

Unladen weight: 1050 kg (2315 lb).

Notes: Standard equipment includes reclining seats, fabric upholstery, centre console, head restraints and halogen headlamps.

RENAULT (F) 20 TX

Identification: Top model in 20-series range of saloons, supplementing TL, LS and TS petrol-engined models and TD and DTD diesels and with equipment specification close to that of 30 TX model.

Engine: Front-mounted four-cylinder in-line with belt-driven overhead camshaft and Weber carburettor. Bore × stroke 88 × 89 mm, displacement 2165 cc. Output 83 kW (115 bhp) @ 5500 rpm, torque 177 Nm (126 lb ft) @ 3000 rpm.

Transmission: Single-disc diaphragm clutch and five-speed manual gearbox, three-speed automatic transmission optional extra. Front-wheel drive.

Suspension: Front, independent with wishbones, coil springs, telescopic shock absorbers and anti-roll bar. Rear, independent with wishbones, coil springs, telescopic shock absorbers and anti-roll bar.

Steering: Rack and pinion, power-assisted.

Brakes: Discs front, drums rear, servo-assisted.

Tyres: 190 HR–14.

Dimensions: Length 4520 mm (178 in), width 1727 mm (68 in), height 1422 mm (56 in), wheelbase 2667 mm (105 in).

Unladen weight: 1295 kg (2854 lb).

Notes: Standard equipment includes alloy wheels, cruise control, electric front window lifts, central door locking, rear screen wash/wipe, tinted glass and front and rear head restraints.

ROLLS-ROYCE (GB)　　　　**Silver Spirit**

Identification: Standard-specification version of model to replace former Silver Shadow II saloon, also available in longer-wheelbase form as Silver Spur with Everflex roof covering and special interior trim.

Engine: Front-mounted V-8-cylinder with pushrod-operated overhead valves and twin SU carburettors. Bore × stroke 104.1 × 99.1 mm, displacement 6750 cc. Output and torque undisclosed.

Transmission: Three-speed automatic transmission. Rear-wheel drive.

Suspension: Front, independent with wishbones, coil springs, telescopic shock absorbers and anti-roll bar. Rear, independent with trailing arms, coil springs, auxiliary gas springs, strut-type shock absorbers and anti-roll bar. Self-levelling.

Steering: Rack and pinion, power-assisted.

Brakes: Ventilated discs front, discs rear, power-assisted.

Tyres: 235/70 HR–15.

Dimensions: Length 5278 mm (207.8 in), width 1887 mm (74.3 in), height 1485 mm (58.5 in), wheelbase 3061 mm (120.5 in).

Unladen weight: 2245 kg (4948 lb).

Notes: Standard equipment includes air-conditioning, headlamp wash/wipe, electrically operated gear selection, front seat adjustment, windows, mirrors, central locking, fuel-filler cap and aerial and stereo radio/cassette player with four speakers.

ROLLS-ROYCE (GB)   Silver Spirit (USA)

Identification: North American version, differing from other-market specification with revised front and rear bumpers, dual headlamps, fuel-injection in place of carburettors and lack of front air dam.

Engine: Front-mounted V-8-cylinder with pushrod-operated overhead valves and Bosch K-Jetronic fuel injection. Bore × stroke 104.1 × 99.1 mm, displacement 6750 cc. Output and torque undisclosed.

Transmission: Three-speed automatic transmission. Rear-wheel drive.

Suspension: Front, independent with wishbones, coil springs, telescopic shock absorbers and anti-roll bar. Rear, independent with trailing arms, coil springs, auxiliary gas springs, strut-type shock absorbers and anti-roll bar. Self-levelling.

Steering: Rack and pinion, power-assisted.

Brakes: Ventilated discs front, discs rear, power-assisted.

Tyres: 235/70 HR-15.

Dimensions: Length 5278 mm (207.8 in), width 1887 mm (74.3 in), height 1485 mm (58.5 in), wheelbase 3061 mm (120.5 in).

Unladen weight: Approximately 2250 kg (4960 lb).

Notes: Standard equipment includes air-conditioning, electrically operated gear selection, front seat adjustment, windows, mirrors, central locking, fuel-filler cap and aerial and stereo radio/cassette player with four speakers.

ROLLS-ROYCE (GB)

Phantom VI

Identification: Most formal model in Rolls-Royce range incorporating similar engine to that used on other models, but allied to more traditional chassis specification.

Engine: Front-mounted V-8-cylinder with pushrod-operated overhead valves and Solex four-choke carburettor. Bore × stroke 104.1 × 99.1 mm, displacement 6750 cc. Output and torque undisclosed.

Transmission: Three-speed automatic transmission. Rear-wheel drive.

Suspension: Front, independent with wishbones, coil springs, lever-type shock absorbers and anti-roll bar. Rear, live axle with semi-elliptic springs and electrically adjustable lever-type shock absorbers.

Steering: Cam and roller, power-assisted.

Brakes: Drums front and rear, power-assisted.

Tyres: 8.90 S–15.

Dimensions: Length 6045 mm (238 in), width 2007 mm (79 in) height 1753 mm (69 in), wheelbase 3660 mm (144.1 in).

Unladen weight: 2742 kg (6045 lb).

Notes: Standard equipment includes seven seats, electric division, air-conditioning, central locking and wide choice of interior materials and equipment.

ROVER (GB)   Vanden Plas

Identification: Top model in revised SD1 range of five-door hatchback saloons, supplementing 2300, 2300S, 2600S and 3500SE models.

Engine: Front-mounted V-8-cylinder with pushrod-operated overhead valves and twin SU carburettors. Bore × stroke 88.9 × 71.1 mm, displacement 3528 cc. Output 116 kW (155 bhp) @ 5250 rpm, torque 268 Nm (198 lb ft) @ 2500 rpm.

Transmission: Single-disc diaphragm clutch and five-speed manual gearbox or three-speed automatic transmission. Rear-wheel drive.

Suspension: Front, independent with MacPherson struts, coil springs, telescopic shock absorbers and anti-roll bar. Rear, live axle with torque tube, coil springs and self-levelling shock absorber units.

Steering: Rack and pinion, power-assisted.

Brakes: Discs front, drums rear, servo-assisted.

Tyres: 195/70 HR–14.

Dimensions: Length 4698 mm (185 in), width 1768 mm (69.6 in), height 1382 mm (54.5 in), wheelbase 2815 mm (110.8 in).

Unladen weight: 1405 kg (3098 lb).

Notes: Standard equipment includes alloy wheels, cruise control, leather upholstery, stereo radio/cassette player, electric sliding roof and window lifts, central locking and tinted glass.

SAAB (S)   900 GL 3-door

Identification: Lowest-priced model in 900 range of three, four and five-door saloons, supplementing more fully equipped GLS and GLE versions and using three-door body also available as 900 Turbo.

Engine: Front-mounted four-cylinder in-line with chain-driven overhead camshaft and Zenith-Stromberg carburettor. Bore × stroke 90 × 78 mm, displacement 1985 cc. Output 75 kW (100 bhp) @ 5200 rpm, torque 165 Nm (119 lb ft) @ 3500 rpm.

Transmission: Single-disc diaphragm clutch and four-speed manual gearbox. Front-wheel drive.

Suspension: Front, independent with wishbones, coil springs and telescopic shock absorbers. Rear, dead axle with four links, Panhard rod, coil springs and telescopic shock absorbers.

Steering: Rack and pinion.

Brakes: Discs front and rear, servo-assisted.

Tyres: 165 SR–15.

Dimensions: Length 4739 mm (186.6 in), width 1690 mm (66.5 in), height 1420 mm (55.9 in), wheelbase 2525 mm (99.4 in).

Unladen weight: 1150 kg (2535 lb).

Notes: Standard equipment includes height-adjustable driver's seat, remote-control door mirrors, anti-theft gear lock, headlamp wash/wipe, folding rear seat and removable parcels shelf.

SAAB (S)   900 Turbo Automatic 5-door

Identification: Development of manual-transmission 900 Turbo, also available with four-door notchback bodywork or as Finnish-built long-wheelbase four-door 900 CD.

Engine: Front-mounted four-cylinder in-line with chain-driven overhead camshaft, Garrett AiResearch exhaust-driven turbo-charger and Bosch fuel injection. Bore × stroke 90 × 78 mm, displacement 1985 cc. Output 108 kW (145 bhp) @ 5000 rpm, torque 240 Nm (174 lb ft) @ 3000 rpm.

Transmission: Three-speed automatic transmission. Front-wheel drive.

Suspension: Front, independent with wishbones, coil springs and telescopic shock absorbers. Rear, dead axle with four longitudinal links, Panhard rod, coil springs and telescopic shock absorbers.

Steering: Rack and pinion, power-assisted.

Brakes: Discs front and rear, servo-assisted.

Tyres: 180/65 HR–390.

Dimensions: Length 4740 mm (186.6 in), width 1690 mm (66.5 in), height 1420 mm (55.9 in), wheelbase 2525 mm (99.4 in).

Unladen weight: 1280 kg (2821 lb).

Notes: Standard equipment includes folding rear seat, halogen headlamps, tinted glass, heated front seats and electrically controlled door mirrors.

SAAB (F) 900 CD

Identification: Longer-wheelbase derivative of 900 Turbo four-door saloon with automatic transmission and manufactured in limited quantities at company's Finnish factory.

Engine: Front-mounted four-cylinder in-line with chain-driven overhead camshaft, Garrett AiResearch exhaust-driven turbocharger and Bosch fuel injection. Bore × stroke 90 × 78 mm, displacement 1985 cc. Output 108 kW (145 bhp) @ 5000 rpm, torque 240 Nm (174 lb ft) @ 3000 rpm.

Transmission: Three-speed automatic transmission. Front-wheel drive.

Suspension: Front, independent with wishbones, coil springs and telescopic shock absorbers. Rear, dead axle with four longitudinal links, Panhard rod, coil springs and telescopic shock absorbers.

Steering: Rack and pinion, power-assisted.

Brakes: Discs front and rear, servo-assisted.

Tyres: 180/65 HR–390.

Dimensions: Length 4940 mm (194.5 in), width 1600 mm (66.5 in), height 1420 mm (55.9 in), wheelbase 2725 mm (107.3 in).

Unladen weight: 1310 kg (2887 lb).

Notes: Standard equipment includes halogen headlamps, tinted glass, heated front seats, electrically controlled door mirrors, individual reading lights, foot cushions and provision for rear radio/telephone console.

SUBARU (J)

1800 GLF 5-speed

Identification: Addition to Subaru saloon range, combining new 1.8-litre engine with improved transmission and supplementing 1600 DL model.

Engine: Front-mounted four-cylinder horizontally opposed with pushrod-operated overhead valves and Hitachi carburettor. Bore × stroke 92 × 67 mm, displacement 1781 cc. Output 59 kW (79 bhp) @ 5200 rpm, torque 135 Nm (98 lb ft) @ 2400 rpm.

Transmission: Single-disc diaphragm clutch and five-speed manual gearbox, three-speed automatic transmission optional extra. Front-wheel drive.

Suspension: Front, independent with MacPherson struts, coil springs, telescopic shock absorbers and anti-roll bar. Rear, independent with trailing arms, torsion bars and telescopic shock absorbers.

Steering: Rack and pinion, power-assistance optional extra.

Brakes: Discs front, drums rear, servo-assisted.

Tyres: 155 SR–13.

Dimensions: Length 4155 mm (163.6 in), width 1615 mm (63.6 in), height 1365 mm (53.7 in), wheelbase 2460 mm (96.9 in).

Unladen weight: 920 kg (2029 lb).

Notes: Standard equipment includes fabric upholstery, reclining seats, tinted glass, radio, warning lamp display and frameless side windows.

SUBARU (J) 1800 GL 4WD Estate

Identification: Addition to Subaru estate range incorporating new 1.8-litre engine, detail styling changes and revised interior and augmenting two-wheel-drive 1600 DL model.

Engine: Front-mounted four-cylinder horizontally opposed with pushrod-operated overhead valves and Hitachi carburettor. Bore × stroke 92 × 67 mm, displacement 1781 cc. Output 59 kW (79 bhp) @ 5200 rpm, torque 135 Nm (98 lb ft) @ 2400 rpm.

Transmission: Single-disc diaphragm clutch and four-speed manual gearbox. Front-wheel or dual-range four-wheel drive.

Suspension: Front, independent with MacPherson struts, coil springs, telescopic shock absorbers and anti-roll bar. Rear, independent with trailing arms, torsion bars and telescopic shock absorbers.

Steering: Rack and pinion.

Brakes: Discs front, drums rear, servo-assisted.

Tyres: 155 SR–13 or 155R–13C–6PR.

Dimensions: Length 4275 mm (168.3 in), width 1620 mm (63.8 in), height 1445 mm (56.9 in), wheelbase 2445 mm (96.3 in).

Unladen weight: 1025 kg (2260 lb).

Notes: Standard equipment includes fabric upholstery, reclining seats, front head restraints, rear screen wash/wipe, radio, rear quarter pocket and painted eight-spoke wheels.

SUZUKI (J)   Alto FX

Identification: Four-door saloon addition to Suzuki range, supplementing two-door SC 100 coupe and powered by new three-cylinder four-stroke water-cooled engine.

Engine: Front and transverse-mounted three-cylinder in-line with belt-driven overhead camshaft and Mikuni carburettor. Bore × stroke 68.5 × 72 mm, displacement 796 cc. Output 29 kW (40 bhp) @ 5500 rpm, torque 59 Nm (43 lb ft) @ 3000 rpm.

Transmission: Single-disc diaphragm clutch and four-speed manual gearbox. Front-wheel drive.

Suspension: Front, independent with MacPherson struts, coil springs and telescopic shock absorbers. Rear, dead axle with semi-elliptic springs and telescopic shock absorbers.

Steering: Rack and pinion.

Brakes: Discs front, drums rear.

Tyres: 145/70 SR–12.

Dimensions: Length 3295 mm (129.7 in), width 1395 mm (54.9 in), height 1335 mm (52.6 in), wheelbase 2150 mm (84.7 in).

Unladen weight: 630 kg (1389 lb).

Notes: Standard equipment includes reclining front seats with head restraints, split rear seat, radio, electric screen washer, trip meter and full carpeting.

TALBOT (GB)   Horizon GLS 1.5

Identification: High-specification model in range of five-door hatchback saloons bridging gap between GL and SX versions and featuring uprated 1.4-litre engine.

Engine: Front and transverse-mounted four-cylinder in-line with pushrod-operated overhead valves and Weber carburettor. Bore × stroke 76.7 × 78 mm, displacement 1442 cc. Output 61 kW (82 bhp) @ 5600 rpm, torque 126 Nm (91 lb ft) @ 3000 rpm.

Transmission: Single-disc diaphragm clutch and four-speed manual gearbox. Front-wheel drive.

Suspension: Front, independent with wishbones, torsion bars, telescopic shock absorbers and anti-roll bar. Rear, independent with trailing arms, transverse torsion bars, telescopic shock absorbers and anti-roll bar.

Steering: Rack and pinion.

Brakes: Discs front, drums rear, servo-assisted.

Tyres: 155 SR–13.

Dimensions: Length 3960 mm (155.9 in), width 1680 mm (66.1 in), height 1410 mm (55.5 in), wheelbase 2520 mm (99.2 in).

Unladen weight: 975 kg (2149 lb).

Notes: Standard equipment includes fabric upholstery, head restraints, radio/stereo cassette player, linear speedometer, laminated screen, rear screen wash/wipe and halogen headlamps.

TALBOT (F)   Matra Murena 2.2

Identification: Two-door coupe based on steel monocoque structure with glass-fibre body panels and incorporating three-across seating. Also available in 1.6-litre form, identifiable by 13-inch diameter steel wheels.

Engine: Centrally and transverse-mounted four-cylinder in-line with chain-driven overhead camshaft and Solex twin-choke carburettor. Bore × stroke 91.7 × 81.6 mm, displacement 2156 cc. Output 88 kW (118 bhp) @ 5800 rpm, torque 192 Nm (139 lb ft) @ 3200 rpm.

Transmission: Single-disc diaphragm clutch and five-speed manual gearbox. Rear-wheel drive.

Suspension: Front, independent with wishbones, torsion bars, telescopic shock absorbers and anti-roll bar. Rear, independent with trailing arms, coil springs, telescopic shock absorbers and anti-roll bar.

Steering: Rack and pinion.

Brakes: Discs front and rear, servo-assisted.

Tyres: 185/60 HR–14 front, 195/60 HR–14 rear.

Dimensions: Length 4070 mm (160.2 in), width 1752 mm (69 in), height 1220 mm (48 in), wheelbase 2435 mm (95.9 in).

Unladen weight: 1050 kg (2314 lb).

Notes: Standard equipment includes front and rear luggage compartments, dual headlamps and galvanized zinc plating of body structure.

TALBOT (GB)   Alpine SX

Identification: Top model in range of five-door hatchback saloons augmenting 1.3-litre LS and 1.4-litre GL and GLS versions and featuring extensive standard equipment.

Engine: Front and transverse-mounted four-cylinder in-line with pushrod-operated overhead valves and Weber twin-choke carburettor. Bore × stroke 80.6 × 78 mm, displacement 1592 cc. Output 64 kW (87 bhp) @ 5400 rpm, torque 141 Nm (101 lb ft) @ 3000 rpm.

Transmission: Single-disc diaphragm clutch and five-speed manual gearbox, three-speed automatic transmission optional extra. Front-wheel drive.

Suspension: Front, independent with wishbones, torsion bars, telescopic shock absorbers and anti-roll bar. Rear, independent with trailing arms, coil springs, telescopic shock absorbers and anti-roll bar.

Steering: Rack and pinion, power-assisted.

Brakes: Discs front, drums rear, servo-assisted.

Tyres: 165 SR–13.

Dimensions: Length 4318 mm (170 in), width 1680 mm (66.1 in), height 1390 mm (54.7 in), wheelbase 2604 mm (102.5 in).

Unladen weight: 1110 kg (2447 lb).

Notes: Standard equipment includes velour upholstery, head restraints, radio/stereo cassette player, electric window lifts, central locking, headlamp wash/wipe and rear screen wash/wipe.

TALBOT (GB)   Solara SX

Identification: Top model in range of four-door saloons derived from Alpine five-door hatchback design, supplementing 1.3-litre LS and 1.6-litre GL and GLS versions.

Engine: Front and transverse-mounted four-cylinder in line with pushrod-operated overhead valves and Weber twin-choke carburettor. Bore × stroke 80.6 × 78 mm, displacement 1592 cc. Output 64 kW (87 bhp) @ 5400 rpm, torque 141 Nm (101 lb ft) @ 3000 rpm.

Transmission: Single-disc diaphragm clutch and five-speed manual gearbox, three-speed automatic transmission optional extra. Front-wheel drive.

Suspension: Front, independent with wishbones, torsion bars, telescopic shock absorbers and anti-roll bar. Rear, independent with trailing arms, coil springs, telescopic shock absorbers and anti-roll bar.

Steering: Rack and pinion, power-assisted.

Brakes: Discs front, drums rear, servo-assisted.

Tyres: 165 SR–13.

Dimensions: Length 4393 mm (173 in), width 1680 mm (66.1 in), height 1390 mm (54.7 in), wheelbase 2604 mm (102.5 in).

Unladen weight: 1095 kg (2414 lb).

Notes: Standard equipment includes velour upholstery, head restraints, electric window lifts, central locking, headlamp wash/wipe, tinted glass and on-board trip computer.

TALBOT (F)   Tagora 2.2 GL

Identification: Least expensive model in range of four-door saloons embracing 2.2-litre four-cylinder and 2.6-litre V-6 engines and GL, GLS and SX levels of trim and equipment.

Engine: Front-mounted four-cylinder in-line with chain-driven overhead camshaft and Solex carburettor. Bore × stroke 91.7 × 81.6 mm, displacement 2155 cc. Output 86 kW (115 bhp) @ 5400 rpm, torque 184 Nm (133 lb ft) @ 3200 rpm.

Transmission: Single-disc diaphragm clutch and four-speed manual gearbox, five-speed manual gearbox optional extra. Rear-wheel drive.

Suspension: Front, independent with MacPherson struts, coil springs, lower links, telescopic shock absorbers and anti-roll bar. Rear, independent with trailing arms, coil springs, telescopic shock absorbers and anti-roll bar.

Steering: Rack and pinion, power assistance optional extra.

Brakes: Discs front, drums rear, servo-assisted.

Tyres: 175 SR–14.

Dimensions: Length 4628 mm (182.2 in), width 1810 mm (71.3 in), height 1444 mm (56.9 in), wheelbase 2808 mm (110.6 in).

Unladen weight: 1255 kg (2766 lb).

Notes: Standard equipment includes dual halogen headlamps, interior headlamp levelling control, radio, twin remote-control exterior mirrors and brake fluid and pad wear warning lights.

TALBOT (F)

Tagora 2.7 SX

Identification: High-performance model of Tagora range incorporating V-6 engine, uprated suspension and brakes and alloy wheels with low-profile tyres.

Engine: Front-mounted V-6-cylinder with chain driven overhead camshafts and twin Weber carburettors. Bore × stroke 88 × 73 mm, displacement 2664 cc. Output 123 kW (165 bhp) @ 6600 rpm, torque 234 Nm (169 lb ft) @ 4200 rpm.

Transmission: Single-disc diaphragm clutch and five-speed manual gearbox, three-speed automatic transmission optional extra. Rear-wheel drive.

Suspension: Front, independent with MacPherson struts, coil springs, lower links, telescopic shock absorbers and anti-roll bar. Rear, independent with trailing arms, coil springs, telescopic shock absorbers and anti roll bar.

Steering: Rack and pinion, power-assisted.

Brakes: Ventilated discs front, discs rear, servo-assisted.

Tyres: 210/65 R365.

Dimensions: Length 4628 mm (182.2 in), width 1810 mm (71.3 in), height 1444 mm (56.9 in), wheelbase 2808 mm (110.6 in).

Unladen weight: 1345 kg (2965 lb).

Notes: Standard equipment includes electrically operated window lifts, height-adjustable driver's seat, contoured seats, trip computer showing instantaneous fuel consumption, voltmeter and oil-pressure gauge.

TOYOTA (J)   Carina 1800 GL

Identification: Top model in revised Carina range, supplementing 1.6-litre-engined DX models and incorporating uprated transmission.

Engine: Front-mounted four-cylinder in-line with pushrod-operated overhead valves and Aisan carburettor. Bore × stroke 85 × 70 mm, displacement 1770 cc. Output 65 kW (86 bhp) @ 5400 rpm, torque 148 Nm (107 lb ft) @ 3600 rpm.

Transmission: Single-disc diaphragm clutch and five-speed manual gearbox, three-speed automatic transmission optional extra. Rear-wheel drive.

Suspension: Front, independent with MacPherson struts, coil springs, telescopic shock absorbers and anti-roll bar. Rear, live axle with four links, Panhard rod, coil springs and telescopic shock absorbers.

Steering: Recirculating ball.

Brakes: Discs front, drums rear, servo-assisted.

Tyres: 165 SR–13.

Dimensions: Length 4330 mm (170.5 in), width 1620 mm (64.2 in), height 1394 mm (54.9 in), wheelbase 2500 mm (98.4 in).

Unladen weight: 1015 kg (2235 lb).

Notes: Standard equipment includes fabric upholstery, head restraints, tinted glass, quartz clock, radio, integral front spoiler and bumper protection pads.

TOYOTA (J)   Cressida DX Diesel

Identification: 2.2-litre diesel-engined alternative to 2-litre petrol-engined Cressida DX saloon incorporating power-assisted steering and other minor specification changes.

Engine: Front-mounted four-cylinder in-line with belt-driven overhead camshaft and Bosch diesel injection. Bore × stroke 90 × 86 mm, displacement 2188 cc. Output 48 kW (60 bhp) @ 4200 rpm, torque 135 Nm (98 lb ft) @ 2400 rpm.

Transmission: Single-disc diaphragm clutch and five-speed manual gearbox. Rear-wheel drive.

Suspension: Front, independent with MacPherson struts, coil springs, telescopic shock absorbers and anti-roll bar. Rear, live axle with four links, Panhard rod, coil springs and telescopic shock absorbers.

Steering: Recirculating ball, power-assisted.

Brakes: Ventilated discs front, drums rear, servo-assisted.

Tyres: 175 SR–14.

Dimensions: Length 4640 mm (182.7 in), width 1690 mm (66.5 in), height 1445 mm (56.9 in), wheelbase 2644 mm (104.1 in).

Unladen weight: 1175 kg (2590 lb).

Notes: Standard equipment includes radio, electric aerial, tinted glass, halogen headlamps and twin door mirrors.

TOYOTA (J)   Cressida GL

Identification: Most luxurious model in revised range of Cressida saloons and estate cars, supplementing petrol and diesel-engined DX models.

Engine: Front-mounted four-cylinder in-line with belt-driven overhead camshaft and Aisan twin-choke carburettor. Bore × stroke 84 × 89 mm, displacement 1972 cc. Output 77 kW (104 bhp) @ 5200 rpm, torque 160 Nm (116 lb ft) @ 3600 rpm.

Transmission: Single-disc diaphragm clutch and five-speed manual gearbox, three-speed automatic transmission optional extra. Rear-wheel drive.

Suspension: Front, independent with MacPherson struts, coil springs, telescopic shock absorbers and anti-roll bar. Rear, live axle with four links, Panhard rod, coil springs and telescopic shock absorbers.

Steering: Rack and pinion.

Brakes: Ventilated discs front, drums rear, servo-assisted.

Tyres: 185/70 HR–14.

Dimensions: Length 4640 mm (182.7 in), width 1600 mm (00.5 in), height 1445 mm (56.9 in), wheelbase 2644 mm (104.1 in).

Unladen weight: 1140 kg (2515 lb).

Notes: Standard equipment includes alloy wheels, headlamp washers, electrically operated sliding roof and window lifts and map-reading lamp.

TOYOTA (J)   Cressida DX Estate

Identification: Five-door model in rebodied and re-engined Cressida range, supplementing petrol-engined and diesel-engined saloons and featuring coil-spring rear suspension.

Engine: Front-mounted four-cylinder in-line with belt-driven overhead camshaft and Aisan twin-choke carburettor. Bore × stroke 84 × 89 mm, displacement 1972 cc. Output 77 kW (104 bhp) @ 5200 rpm, torque 160 Nm (116 lb ft) @ 3600 rpm.

Transmission: Single-disc diaphragm clutch and five-speed manual gearbox. Rear-wheel drive.

Suspension: Front, independent with MacPherson struts, coil springs, telescopic shock absorbers and anti-roll bar. Rear, live axle with four links, Panhard rod, coil springs and telescopic shock absorbers.

Steering: Rack and pinion.

Brakes: Ventilated discs front, drums rear, servo-assisted.

Tyres: 175 SR–14.

Dimensions: Length 4647 mm (182.9 in), width 1690 mm (66.5 in), height 1473 mm (58 in), wheelbase 2644 mm (104.1 in).

Unladen weight: 1140 kg (2515 lb).

Notes: Standard equipment includes electric tailgate lock, rear screen wash/wipe, height-adjustable driver's seat and two-way adjustable head restraints.

167

TOYOTA (J)   Land Cruiser

Identification: Five-door estate version of range of four-wheel-drive off-road vehicles powered by diesel engine and incorporating higher level of interior equipment.

Engine: Front-mounted six-cylinder in-line with pushrod-operated overhead valves and Bosch diesel injection. Bore × stroke 91 × 102 mm, displacement 3980 cc. Output 76 kW (102 bhp) @ 3500 rpm, torque 128 Nm (177 lb ft) @ 2300 rpm.

Transmission: Single-disc diaphragm clutch and four-speed manual gearbox with two-speed transfer box. Four-wheel drive.

Suspension: Front, rigid axle with leaf springs, telescopic shock absorbers and anti-roll bar. Rear, rigid axle with leaf springs and telescopic shock absorbers.

Steering: Recirculating ball, power-assisted.

Brakes: Ventilated discs front, drums rear, servo-assisted.

Tyres: 205 SR–16.

Dimensions: Length 4675 mm (184.1 in), width 1800 mm (70.9 in), height 1815 mm (71.5 in), wheelbase 2730 mm (107.5 in).

Unladen weight: 1970 kg (4343 lb).

Notes: Standard equipment includes fabric upholstery, adjustable front head restraints, tilting steering wheel, two-part tailgate, dashboard-mounted hand throttle for 'crawler' operations, oil inter-cooler and 24-volt electrical system.

TRIUMPH (GB)   Acclaim HLS

Identification: Intermediate model in new range of four-door saloons based on Honda Ballade and bridging gap between similarly powered HL and CD models.

Engine: Front and transverse-mounted four-cylinder in-line with belt-driven overhead camshaft and twin Keihin carburettors. Bore × stroke 72 × 82 mm, displacement 1335 cc. Output 52 kW (70 bhp) @ 5750 rpm, torque 100 Nm (74 lb ft) @ 3500 rpm.

Transmission: Single-disc diaphragm clutch and five-speed manual gearbox, three-speed semi-automatic transmission optional extra. Front-wheel drive.

Suspension: Front, independent with MacPherson struts, coil springs, telescopic shock absorbers and anti-roll bar. Rear, independent with trailing and transverse arms, MacPherson struts, coil springs and telescopic shock absorbers.

Steering: Rack and pinion.

Brakes: Discs front, drums rear, servo-assisted.

Tyres: 155 SR–13.

Dimensions: Length 4095 mm (161.2 in), width 1600 mm (63 in), height 1340 mm (52.7 in), wheelbase 2320 mm (91.3 in).

Unladen weight: 815 kg (1797 lb).

Notes: Standard equipment includes velour upholstery, rear seat boot hatch, tinted glass, halogen headlamps, remote-control door mirrors and interior fuel filler cap release.

TRIUMPH (GB)   Acclaim CD

Identification: Top model in range of four-door saloons based on Honda Ballade and supplementing HL and HLS models with similar mechanical equipment but simpler trim.

Engine: Front and transverse-mounted four-cylinder in-line with belt-driven overhead camshaft and twin Keihin carburettors. Bore × stroke 72 × 82 mm, displacement 1335 cc. Output 52 kW (70 bhp) @ 5750 rpm, torque 100 Nm (74 lb ft) @ 3500 rpm.

Transmission: Single-disc diaphragm clutch and five-speed manual gearbox, three-speed semi-automatic transmission optional extra. Front-wheel drive.

Suspension: Front, independent with MacPherson struts, coil springs, telescopic shock absorbers and anti-roll bar. Rear, independent with trailing and transverse arms, MacPherson struts, coil springs and telescopic shock absorbers.

Steering: Rack and pinion.

Brakes: Discs front, drums rear, servo-assisted.

Tyres: 165/70 SR–13.

Dimensions: Length 4095 mm (161.2 in), width 1600 mm (63 in), height 1340 mm (52.7 in), wheelbase 2320 mm (91.3 in).

Unladen weight: 825 kg (1819 lb).

Notes: Standard equipment includes electric window lifts, headlamp washers, head restraints, radio/stereo cassette player and carpeted luggage compartment.

TVR (GB)   Tasmin 200

Identification: Addition to Tasmin range, supplementing 2.8-litre models and powered by 2-litre Ford Capri engine and available with open or closed coupe bodywork.

Engine: Front-mounted four-cylinder in-line with belt-driven overhead camshaft and Weber carburettor. Bore × stroke 90.8 × 77 mm, displacement 1993 cc. Output 72 kW (96 bhp) @ 5200 rpm, torque 151 Nm (109 lb ft) @ 3500 rpm.

Transmission: Single-disc diaphragm clutch and four-speed manual gearbox. Rear-wheel drive.

Suspension: Front, independent with wishbones, coil springs, telescopic shock absorbers and anti-roll bar. Rear, independent with trailing arms, fixed-length drive shafts, coil springs and telescopic shock absorbers.

Steering: Rack and pinion.

Brakes: Discs front and rear, servo-assisted.

Tyres: 185/65 HR–14.

Dimensions: Length 4013 mm (158 in), width 1727 mm (68 in), height 1191 mm (46.9 in), wheelbase 2388 mm (94 in).

Unladen weight: 1025 kg (2259 lb).

Notes: Standard equipment includes head restraints, full carpeting, matt-finished dashboard, full door trim, centre console and halogen headlamps.

VAUXHALL (GB)

Astra L Estate

Identification: Five-door estate version of 1.3-litre range of Astra models, supplementing three-door and five-door hatchback models in L or GL trim.

Engine: Front and transverse-mounted four-cylinder in-line with belt-driven overhead camshaft and GM carburettor. Bore × stroke 75 × 73.4 mm, displacement 1297 cc. Output 55 kW (75 bhp) @ 5800 rpm, torque 103 Nm (74 lb ft) @ 3800 rpm.

Transmission: Single-disc diaphragm clutch and four-speed manual gearbox. Front-wheel drive.

Suspension: Front, independent with MacPherson struts, coil springs, telescopic shock absorbers and anti-roll bar. Rear, dead axle with trailing arms, coil springs, telescopic shock absorbers and anti-roll bar.

Steering: Rack and pinion.

Brakes: Discs front, drums rear, servo-assisted.

Tyres: 155 SR–13.

Dimensions: Length 4210 mm (165.7 in), width 1638 mm (64.5 in), height 1400 mm (55.1 in), wheelbase 2515 mm (99 in).

Unladen weight: 905 kg (1995 lb).

Notes: Standard equipment includes centre console, fabric upholstery, head restraints, rear screen wash/wipe and load-bearing spare wheel cover.

VAUXHALL (GB)   Cavalier

Identification: Two-door base model in Vauxhall version of GM J-car range comprising two-door and four-door saloons and five-door hatchbacks and 1.3-litre or 1.6-litre engines.

Engine: Front and transverse-mounted four-cylinder in-line with belt-driven overhead camshaft and GM carburettor. Bore × stroke 75 × 73.4 mm, displacement 1297 cc. Output 56 kW (75 bhp) @ 5800 rpm, torque 103 Nm (74 lb ft) @ 3800 rpm.

Transmission: Single-disc diaphragm clutch and four-speed manual gearbox. Front-wheel drive.

Suspension: Front, independent with MacPherson struts, coil springs, telescopic shock absorbers and anti-roll bar. Rear, semi-independent with trailing arms, torsion beam, coil springs, telescopic shock absorbers and anti-roll bar.

Steering: Rack and pinion.

Brakes: Discs front, drums rear, servo-assisted.

Tyres: 155 SR–13.

Dimensions: Length 4366 mm (171.9 in), width 1668 mm (65.7 in), height 1395 mm (54.9 in), wheelbase 2574 mm (101.3 in).

Unladen weight: 940 kg (2116 lb).

Notes: Standard equipment includes reclining seats, head restraints, fabric upholstery, centre console, glove box, carpeted luggage compartment and locking fuel filler cap.

VAUXHALL (GB)   Cavalier GL 1600

Identification: Intermediate model in four-door saloon sector of J-car range, bridging gap between L and GLS versions and also available with 1.3-litre engine.

Engine: Front and transverse-mounted four-cylinder in-line with belt-driven overhead camshaft and GM carburettor. Bore × stroke 80 × 79.5 mm, displacement 1598 cc. Output 67 kW (90 bhp) @ 5800 rpm, torque 129 Nm (93 lb ft) @ 3800 rpm.

Transmission: Single-disc diaphragm clutch and four-speed manual gearbox. Front-wheel drive.

Suspension: Front, independent with MacPherson struts, coil springs, telescopic shock absorbers and anti-roll bar. Rear, semi-independent with trailing arms, torsion beam, coil springs, telescopic shock absorbers and anti-roll bar.

Steering: Rack and pinion.

Brakes: Discs front, drums rear, servo-assisted.

Tyres: 165 SR–13.

Dimensions: Length 4366 mm (171.9 in), width 1668 mm (65.7 in), height 1395 mm (54.9 in), wheelbase 2574 mm (101.3 in).

Unladen weight: 1010 kg (2227 lb).

Notes: Standard equipment includes velour upholstery and carpet, engine compartment light, full instrumentation, lights-on warning buzzer and four-spoke steering wheel.

VAUXHALL (GB)   Cavalier GLS Hatch

Identification: High-specification model in hatchback sector of J-car range, supplementing 1.3-litre and 1.6-litre L and GL models and only available with 1.6-litre engine.

Engine: Front and transverse-mounted four-cylinder in-line with belt-driven overhead camshaft and GM carburettor. Bore × stroke 80 × 79.5 mm, displacement 1598 cc. Output 67 kW (90 bhp) @ 5800 rpm, torque 129 Nm (93 lb ft) @ 3800 rpm.

Transmission: Single-disc diaphragm clutch and four-speed manual gearbox. Front-wheel drive.

Suspension: Front, independent with MacPherson struts, coil springs, telescopic shock absorbers and anti-roll bar. Rear, semi-independent with trailing arms, torsion beam, coil springs, telescopic shock absorbers and anti-roll bar.

Steering: Rack and pinion

Brakes: Discs front, drums rear, servo-assisted.

Tyres: 165 SR–13.

Dimensions: Length 4264 mm (167.9 in), width 1668 mm (65.7 in), height 1385 mm (54.5 in), wheelbase 2574 mm (101.3 in).

Unladen weight: 1035 kg (2282 lb).

Notes: Standard equipment includes sliding roof, radio/stereo cassette player, alloy wheels, laminated screen, tinted glass and remote-control passenger's door mirror.

VAUXHALL (GB)   Cavalier SR Hatch

Identification: Sporting model in Cavalier J-car range, also available as four-door saloon with similar mechanical specification and supplementing base, L, GL and GLS 1.6-litre models.

Engine: Front and transverse-mounted four-cylinder in-line with belt-driven overhead camshaft and GM carburettor. Bore × stroke 80 × 79.5 mm, displacement 1598 cc. Output 67 kW (90 bhp) @ 5800 rpm, torque 129 Nm (93 lb ft) @ 3800 rpm.

Transmission: Single-disc diaphragm clutch and four-speed manual gearbox. Front-wheel drive.

Suspension: Front, independent with MacPherson struts, coil springs, telescopic shock absorbers and anti-roll bar. Rear, semi-independent with trailing arms, torsion beam, coil springs, telescopic shock absorbers and anti-roll bar.

Steering: Rack and pinion.

Brakes: Discs front, drums rear, servo-assisted.

Tyres: 195/60 HR–14.

Dimensions: Length 4264 mm (167.9 in), width 1668 mm (65.7 in), height 1385 mm (54.5 in), wheelbase 2574 mm (101.3 in).

Unladen weight: 1035 kg (2282 lb).

Notes: Standard equipment includes Recaro front seats, sports steering wheel, alloy wheels, exterior body stripes and special paint treatment.

VAUXHALL (D)   Viceroy

Identification: Intermediate high-specification executive saloon based on Carlton four-door bodyshell and powered by smaller version of six-cylinder engine used in Royale.

Engine: Front-mounted six-cylinder in-line with chain-driven overhead camshaft and Zenith carburettor. Bore × stroke 87 × 69.8 mm, displacement 2490 cc. Output 85 kW (115 bhp) @ 5200 rpm, torque 179 Nm (132 lb ft) @ 3800 rpm.

Transmission: Single-disc diaphragm clutch and four-speed manual gearbox, overdrive gearbox or three-speed automatic transmission optional extras. Rear-wheel drive.

Suspension: Front, independent with MacPherson struts, coil springs, telescopic shock absorbers and anti-roll bar. Rear, live axle with four-link system, coil springs, telescopic shock absorbers and anti-roll bar.

Steering: Recirculating ball, power-assisted.

Brakes: Discs front, drums rear, servo-assisted.

Tyres: 195/70 HR–14.

Dimensions: Length 4732 mm (186.3 in), width 1722 mm (67.8 in), height 1410 mm (55.5 in), wheelbase 2667 mm (105 in).

Unladen weight: 1220 kg (2690 lb).

Notes: Standard equipment includes velour upholstery, head restraints, radio/cassette player, central locking and height-adjustable driver's seat.

VAUXHALL (D)   Royale 2800 Coupe

Identification: Smaller-engined of two coupe versions of top Vauxhall model, also available in 3-litre fuel-injected form and supplementing four-door saloon models, all based on Opel Senator/Monza range.

Engine: Front-mounted six-cylinder in-line with chain-driven overhead camshaft and Solex carburettor. Bore × stroke 92 × 69.8 mm, displacement 2784 cc. Output 105 kW (140 bhp) @ 5200 rpm, torque 223 Nm (161 lb ft) @ 3400 rpm.

Transmission: Single-disc diaphragm clutch and four-speed manual gearbox or three-speed automatic transmission. Rear-wheel drive.

Suspension: Front, independent with MacPherson struts, coil springs, telescopic shock absorbers and anti-roll bar. Rear, independent with trailing arms, coil springs, telescopic shock absorbers and anti-roll bar.

Steering: Recirculating ball, power-assisted.

Brakes: Ventilated discs front, discs rear, servo-assisted.

Tyres: 195/70 SR–14.

Dimensions: Length 4690 mm (184.7 in), width 1735 mm (68.3 in), height 1334 mm (52.5 in), wheelbase 2667 mm (105 in).

Unladen weight: 1375 kg (3030 lb)

Notes: Standard equipment includes alloy wheels, electric window lifts, sliding roof, tinted glass, velour upholstery and head restraints.

VOLKSWAGEN (D)   Polo CL 1.1

Identification: Intermediate model in completely revised VW Polo range, bridging gap between C and GL models and supplementing similar models with 1.0 and 1.3-litre engines.

Engine: Front and transverse-mounted four-cylinder in-line with belt-driven overhead camshaft and Solex carburettor. Bore × stroke 69.5 × 72 mm, displacement 1093 cc. Output 37 kW (50 bhp) @ 5800 rpm, torque 77 Nm (56 lb ft) @ 3500 rpm.

Transmission: Single-disc diaphragm clutch and four-speed manual gearbox. Front-wheel drive.

Suspension: Front, independent with MacPherson struts, coil springs, telescopic shock absorbers and anti-roll bar. Rear, independent with trailing arms, coil springs and telescopic shock absorbers.

Steering: Rack and pinion.

Brakes: Discs front, drums rear, servo-assisted.

Tyres: 145 SR–13.

Dimensions: Length 3655 mm (143.9 in), width 1580 mm (62.2 in), height 1355 mm (53.4 in), wheelbase 2335 mm (91.9 in).

Unladen weight: 710 kg (1565 lb).

Notes: Standard equipment includes fabric upholstery, head restraints, rear screen wash/wipe, load compartment cover and fold-forward rear seats.

VOLKSWAGEN (D) Derby GL 1.3

Identification: Top model in completely revised VW Derby range also including choice of 1.0 and 1.1-litre engines and C and CL trim levels.

Engine: Front and transverse-mounted four-cylinder in-line with belt-driven overhead camshaft and Solex carburettor. Bore × stroke 75 × 72 mm, displacement 1272 cc. Output 44 kW (60 bhp) @ 5600 rpm, torque 95 Nm (69 lb ft) @ 3500 rpm.

Transmission: Single-disc diaphragm clutch and four-speed manual gearbox. Front-wheel drive.

Suspension: Front, independent with MacPherson struts, coil springs, telescopic shock absorbers and anti-roll bar. Rear, independent with trailing arms, coil springs and telescopic shock absorbers.

Steering: Rack and pinion.

Brakes: Discs front, drums rear, servo-assisted.

Tyres: 145 SR–13.

Dimensions: Length 3975 mm (156.5 in), width 1580 mm (62.2 in), height 1355 mm (53.4 in), wheelbase 2335 mm (91.9 in).

Unladen weight: 735 kg (1620 lb).

Notes: Standard equipment includes fabric upholstery, head restraints, headlamp washers, internally adjustable rear-view mirror and intermittent wipers.

VOLKSWAGEN (D)   Golf GTi

Identification: High-performance model in re-aligned Golf range supplementing C, CL and GL saloons and GL and GLi cabriolets and embracing 1.1, 1.3, 1.5 and 1.6-litre petrol and 1.6-litre diesel engines.

Engine: Front and transverse-mounted four-cylinder in-line with belt-driven overhead camshaft and Bosch K-Jetronic fuel injection. Bore × stroke 79.5 × 80 mm, displacement 1588 cc. Output 81 kW (110 bhp) @ 6100 rpm, torque 140 Nm (101 lb ft) @ 5000 rpm.

Transmission: Single-disc diaphragm clutch and five-speed manual gearbox. Front-wheel drive.

Suspension: Front, independent with MacPherson struts, coil springs, telescopic shock absorbers and anti-roll bar. Rear, independent with trailing arms, torsion bars, coil springs, telescopic shock absorbers and anti-roll bar.

Steering: Rack and pinion.

Brakes: Ventilated discs front, drums rear, servo-assisted.

Tyres: 175/70 HR–13.

Dimensions: Length 3815 mm (150.2 in), width 1630 mm (64.2 in), height 1395 mm (54.9 in), wheelbase 2400 mm (94.5 in).

Unladen weight: 840 kg (1851 lb).

Notes: Standard equipment includes fabric upholstery, head restraints, rear screen wash/wipe, front and rear spoilers, halogen headlamps and windscreen post wind deflectors.

VOLKSWAGEN (D)　　　　　　Jetta GL 1.6

Identification: Intermediate model in re-aligned Jetta range bridging gap between 1.3 and 1.5-litre versions and fuel-injected 1.6 GLi; Jetta C and CL models also available with 1.3, 1.5 and 1.6-litre engines.

Engine: Front and transverse-mounted four-cylinder in-line with belt-driven overhead camshaft and Solex carburettor. Bore × stroke 79.5 × 80 mm, displacement 1588 cc. Output 63 kW (85 bhp) @ 5600 rpm, torque 125 Nm (90 lb ft) @ 3800 rpm.

Transmission: Single-disc diaphragm clutch and five-speed manual gearbox, three-speed automatic transmission optional extra. Front-wheel drive.

Suspension: Front, independent with MacPherson struts, coil springs, telescopic shock absorbers and anti-roll bar. Rear, semi-independent with torsion beam, trailing arms, coil springs, telescopic shock absorbers and anti-roll bar.

Steering: Rack and pinion.

Brakes: Discs front, drums rear, servo-assisted.

Tyres: 175/70 SR–13.

Dimensions: Length 4195 mm (165.2 in), width 1630 mm (64.2 in), height 1410 mm (55.5 in), wheelbase 2400 mm (94.5 in).

Unladen weight: 850 kg (1873 lb).

Notes: Standard equipment includes fabric upholstery, head restraints, headlamp washers, halogen headlamps, internally adjustable rear-view mirror and centre console.

VOLKSWAGEN (D)

Scirocco GT

Identification: Intermediate model in completely restyled VW Scirocco range bridging gap between 1.3 and 1.5-litre CL and GL models and 1.6-litre fuel-injected GLi and GTi versions.

Engine: Front and transverse-mounted four-cylinder in-line with belt-driven overhead camshaft and Solex carburettor. Bore × stroke 79.5 × 80 mm, displacement 1588 cc. Output 64 kW (85 bhp) @ 5600 rpm, torque 125 Nm (90 lb ft) @ 3800 rpm.

Transmission: Single-disc diaphragm clutch and five-speed manual gearbox, three-speed automatic transmission optional extra. Front-wheel drive.

Suspension: Front, independent with MacPherson struts, coil springs, telescopic shock absorbers and anti-roll bar. Rear, independent with trailing arms, torsion bars, coil springs, telescopic shock absorbers and anti-roll bar.

Steering: Rack and pinion.

Brakes: Discs front, drums rear, servo-assisted.

Tyres: 175/70 HR-13.

Dimensions: Length 4050 mm (159.5 in), width 1625 mm (64 in), height 1306 mm (51.4 in), wheelbase 2400 mm (94.5 in).

Unladen weight: 855 kg (1884 lb).

Notes: Standard equipment includes fabric upholstery, head restraints, dual headlamps, headlamp washers, rear spoiler and alloy wheels.

VOLKSWAGEN (D)

Passat LS

Identification: Five-door hatchback saloon version of rebodied Passat, also available as five-door estate car and incorporating significantly increased accommodation over previous model.

Engine: Front-mounted four-cylinder in-line with belt-driven overhead camshaft and Solex carburettor. Bore × stroke 79.5 × 80 mm, displacement 1588 cc. Output 64 kW (85 bhp) @ 5600 rpm, torque 127 Nm (92 lb ft) @ 3200 rpm.

Transmission: Single-disc diaphragm clutch and four-speed manual gearbox, three-speed automatic transmission optional extra. Front-wheel drive.

Suspension: Front, independent with MacPherson struts, coil springs and telescopic shock absorbers. Rear, torsion beam axle with trailing arms, coil springs and telescopic shock absorbers.

Steering: Rack and pinion.

Brakes: Discs front, drums rear, servo-assisted.

Tyres: 165 SR–13.

Dimensions: Length 4435 mm (174.6 in), width 1684 mm (66.3 in), height 1384 mm (54.5 in), wheelbase 2550 mm (100.4 in).

Unladen weight: 955 kg (2106 lb).

Notes: Standard equipment includes fabric upholstery, reclining seats, folding rear seats, halogen headlamps and front and rear seat belts.

VOLKSWAGEN (D)   Passat GL5S

Identification: Higher-powered and more luxuriously equipped alternative to LS saloon in rebodied Passat range, also available as five-door estate car.

Engine: Front-mounted five-cylinder in-line with belt-driven overhead camshaft and twin-choke Solex carburettor. Bore × stroke 79.5 × 77.4 mm, displacement 1921 cc. Output 86 kW (115 bhp) @ 5900 rpm, torque 154 Nm (111 lb ft) @ 3700 rpm.

Transmission: Single-disc diaphragm clutch and five-speed manual gearbox, three-speed automatic transmission optional extra. Front-wheel drive.

Suspension: Front, independent with MacPherson struts, coil springs and telescopic shock absorbers. Rear, torsion beam axle with trailing arms, coil springs and telescopic shock absorbers.

Steering: Rack and pinion, power-assisted.

Brakes: Discs front, drums rear, servo-assisted.

Tyres: 185/70 HR–13.

Dimensions: Length 4435 mm (174.6 in), width 1684 mm (66.3 in), height 1384 mm (54.5 in), wheelbase 2550 mm (100.4 in).

Unladen weight: 1050 kg (2315 lb).

Notes: Standard equipment includes alloy wheels, tinted glass, remote-control door mirrors, digital clock, asymmetrically split rear seat and carpeted luggage compartment.

VOLKSWAGEN (D)   Passat GL5S Estate

Identification: More luxurious of two five-door estate cars in rebodied Passat range, supplementing 1.6-litre LS model and incorporating new five-cylinder in-line engine.

Engine: Front-mounted five-cylinder in-line with belt-driven overhead camshaft and twin-choke Solex carburettor. Bore × stroke 79.5 × 77.4 mm, displacement 1921 cc. Output 86 kW (115 bhp) @ 5900 rpm, torque 154 Nm (111 lb ft) @ 3700 rpm.

Transmission: Single-disc diaphragm clutch and five-speed manual gearbox, three-speed automatic transmission optional extra. Front-wheel drive.

Suspension: Front, independent with MacPherson struts, coil springs, telescopic shock absorbers and anti-roll bar. Rear, torsion beam axle with trailing arms, coil springs and telescopic shock absorbers.

Steering: Rack and pinion, power-assisted.

Brakes: Discs front, drums rear, servo-assisted.

Tyres: 185/70 HR–13.

Dimensions. Length 4539 mm (178.7 in), width 1684 mm (66.3 in), height 1369 mm (53.9 in), wheelbase 2550 mm (100.4 in).

Unladen weight: 1060 kg (2337 lb).

Notes: Standard equipment includes alloy wheels, tinted glass, roof rails, remote-control door mirrors, digital clock, asymmetrically split rear seat and carpeted load compartment.

VOLKSWAGEN (D)   Santana GL 5

Identification: Top model in new range of four-door saloons based on Passat components but offering higher level of trim and equipment, also available with 1.6-litre petrol or diesel engines.

Engine: Front-mounted five-cylinder in-line with belt-driven overhead camshaft and twin-choke Solex carburettor. Bore × stroke 79.5 × 77.4 mm, displacement 1921 cc. Output 86 kW (115 bhp) @ 5900 rpm, torque 154 Nm (111 lb ft) @ 3700 rpm.

Transmission: Single-disc diaphragm clutch and five-speed manual gearbox, three-speed automatic transmission optional extra. Front-wheel drive.

Suspension: Front, independent with MacPherson struts, coil springs and telescopic shock absorbers. Rear, torsion beam axle with trailing arms, coil springs and telescopic shock absorbers.

Steering: Rack and pinion, power-assistance optional extra.

Brakes: Ventilated discs front, drums rear, servo-assisted.

Tyres: 185/70 HR–13.

Dimensions: Length 4545 mm (178.9 in), width 1695 mm (66.7 in), height 1400 mm (55.1 in), wheelbase 2550 mm (100.4 in).

Unladen weight: 1080 kg (2380 lb).

Notes: Standard equipment includes fabric upholstery, head restraints, twin exterior mirrors, headlamp washers, rear passenger console and alloy wheels.

VOLVO (NL)   343 GL

Identification: Latest version of 343, supplementing more simply equipped DL model and incorporating revised frontal styling and other detail changes, also available with five-door bodywork as 345 model.

Engine: Front-mounted four-cylinder in-line with pushrod-operated overhead valves and Weber carburettor. Bore × stroke 76 × 77 mm, displacement 1397 cc. Output 52 kW (70 bhp) @ 5500 rpm, torque 109 Nm (79 lb ft) @ 2500 rpm.

Transmission: Single-disc diaphragm clutch and four-speed manual gearbox, belt-driven automatic transmission optional extra. Rear-wheel drive.

Suspension: Front, independent with MacPherson struts, coil springs, telescopic shock absorbers and anti-roll bar. Rear, de Dion axle with trailing arms, semi-elliptic springs and telescopic shock absorbers.

Steering: Rack and pinion.

Brakes: Discs front, drums rear, servo-assisted.

Tyres: 175/70 SR–13.

Dimensions: Length 4205 mm (165.6 in), width 1660 mm (65.4 in), height 1392 mm (54.8 in), wheelbase 2395 mm (94.3 in).

Unladen weight: 980 kg (2160 lb).

Notes: Standard equipment includes tinted glass, halogen headlamps with wash/wipe, heated driver's seat, reclining seats, head restraints, mud flaps and quartz clock.

VOLVO (S)

Identification: Addition to Volvo estate range incorporating uprated 2.3-litre engine first offered in 244 GLT saloon and augmenting DL, GL and GLE models.

Engine: Front-mounted four-cylinder in-line with belt-driven overhead camshaft and Bosch K-Jetronic fuel injection. Bore × stroke 96 × 80 mm, displacement 2315 cc. Output 102 kW (136 bhp) @ 5500 rpm, torque 190 Nm (140 lb ft) @ 4500 rpm.

Transmission: Single-disc diaphragm clutch and four-speed manual gearbox with overdrive. Rear-wheel drive.

Suspension: Front, independent with MacPherson struts, coil springs, telescopic shock absorbers and anti-roll bar. Rear, live axle with trailing arms, coil springs, telescopic shock absorbers and anti-roll bar.

Steering: Rack and pinion, power assisted.

Brakes: Discs front and rear, servo-assisted.

Tyres: 195/60 HR–15.

Dimensions: Length 4790 mm (188.4 in), width 1710 mm (67.1 in), height 1460 mm (57.5 in), wheelbase 2640 mm (104 in).

Unladen weight: 1310 kg (2887 lb).

Notes: Standard equipment includes alloy wheels, tinted glass, head restraints, headlamp wash/wipe and rear screen wash/wipe.

VOLVO (S)

245 Turbo

Identification: High-performance addition to Volvo four-cylinder estate car range, combining turbocharged version of 2.1-litre engine with high level of chassis and interior equipment.

Engine: Front-mounted four-cylinder in-line with belt-driven overhead camshaft, Bosch K-Jetronic fuel injection and Garrett AiResearch exhaust-driven turbocharger. Bore × stroke 92 × 80 mm, displacement 2127 cc. Output 114 kW (155 bhp) @ 5500 rpm, torque 240 Nm (174 lb ft) @ 3750 rpm.

Transmission: Single-disc diaphragm clutch and five-speed manual gearbox. Rear-wheel drive.

Suspension: Front, independent with MacPherson struts, coil springs, telescopic shock absorbers and anti-roll bar. Rear, live axle with trailing arms, coil springs, telescopic shock absorbers and anti-roll bar.

Steering: Rack and pinion, power-assisted.

Brakes: Ventilated discs front, discs rear, servo-assisted.

Tyres: 195/60 HR–15.

Dimensions: Length 4790 mm (188.4 in), width 1710 mm (67.1 in), height 1430 mm (56.3 in), wheelbase 2650 mm (104.3 in).

Unladen weight: 1390 kg (3064 lb).

Notes: Standard equipment includes fabric upholstery, head restraints, headlamp wash/wipe, rear screen wash/wipe, alloy wheels, mud flaps and internally adjustable rear-view mirrors.

ZASTAVA (YU)   1100 ZLM Mediteran

Identification: New-to-UK three-door version of range of Yugoslavian-built and Fiat 128-derived hatchback saloons offered with choice of 1.1-litre or 1.3 litre engines.

Engine: Front and transverse-mounted four-cylinder in-line with belt-driven overhead camshaft and Weber-style carburettor. Bore × stroke 80 × 55.5 mm, displacement 1116 cc. Output 41 kW (55 bhp) @ 6000 rpm, torque 90 Nm (65 lb ft) @ 3000 rpm.

Transmission: Single-disc diaphragm clutch and four-speed manual gearbox. Front-wheel drive.

Suspension: Front, independent with MacPherson struts, coil springs, telescopic shock absorbers and anti-roll bar. Rear, independent with trailing links, transverse leaf spring and telescopic shock absorbers.

Steering: Rack and pinion.

Brakes: Discs front, drums rear.

Tyres: 145 SR–13.

Dimensions: Length 3792 mm (149.3 in), width 1588 mm (62.5 in), height 1372 mm (54 in), wheelbase 2450 mm (96.5 in).

Unladen weight: 835 kg (1840 lb).

Notes: Standard equipment includes fabric upholstery, folding rear seat, shelf over luggage compartment, adjustable head restraints, electric screen washers and tool and first-aid kits.

Identification: Five-door alternative to three-door Mediteran model with similar mechanical specification, also available as ZLX Special with 1.3-litre engine.

Engine: Front and transverse-mounted four-cylinder in-line with belt-driven overhead camshaft and Weber-style carburettor. Bore × stroke 80 × 55.5 mm, displacement 1116 cc. Output 41 kW (55 bhp) @ 6000 rpm, torque 90 Nm (65 lb ft) @ 3000 rpm.

Transmission: Single-disc diaphragm clutch and four-speed manual gearbox. Front-wheel drive.

Suspension: Front, independent with MacPherson struts, coil springs, telescopic shock absorbers and anti-roll bar. Rear, independent with trailing links, transverse leaf spring and telescopic shock absorbers.

Steering: Rack and pinion.

Brakes: Discs front, drums rear.

Tyres: 145 SR–13.

Dimensions: Length 3792 mm (149.3 in), width 1588 mm (62.5 in), height 1372 mm (54 in), wheelbase 2450 mm (96.5 in).

Unladen weight: 850 kg (1873 lb).

Notes: Standard equipment includes reclining seats with adjustable head restraints, fabric upholstery, load-adjustable headlamps, locking fuel cap, tool and first-aid kits and luggage compartment shelf.